Emigration from Europe 1815–1930

New Studies in Economic and Social History

Edited for the Economic History Society by
Michael Sanderson
University of East Anglia, Norwich

This series, specially commissioned by the Economic History Society, provides a guide to the current interpretations of the key themes of economic and social history in which advances have recently been made or in which there has been significant debate.

In recent times economic and social history has been one of the most flourishing areas of historical study. This has mirrored the increasing relevance of the economic and social sciences both in a student's choice of career and in forming a society at large more aware of the importance of these issues in their everyday lives. Moreover specialist interests in business, agricultural and welfare history, for example, have themselves burgeoned and there has been an increased interest in the economic development of the wider world. Stimulating as these scholarly developments have been for the specialist, the rapid advance of the subject and the quantity of new publications make it difficult for the reader to gain an overview of particular topics, let alone the whole field.

New Studies in Economic and Social History is intended for students and their teachers. It is designed to introduce them to fresh topics and to enable them to keep abreast of recent writing and debates. All the books in the series are written by a recognised authority in the subject, and the arguments and issues are set out in a critical but unpartisan fashion. The aim of the series is to survey the current state of scholarship, rather than to provide a set of prepackaged conclusions.

The series has been edited since its inception in 1968 by Professors M. W. Flinn, T. C. Smout and L. A. Clarkson, and is currently edited by Dr Michael Sanderson. From 1968 it was published by Macmillan as *Studies in Economic History*, and after 1974 as *Studies in Economic and Social History*. From 1995 *New Studies in Economic and Social History* is being published on behalf of the Economic History Society by Cambridge University Press. This new series includes some of the titles previously published by Macmillan as well as new titles, and reflects the ongoing development throughout the world of this rich seam of history.

For a full list of titles in print, please see the end of the book.

Emigration from Europe 1815–1930

Prepared for the Economic History Society by

Dudley Baines
London School of Economics

CAMBRIDGE
UNIVERSITY PRESS

Published by the Press Syndicate of the University of Cambridge
The Pitt Building, Trumpington Street, Cambridge CB2 1RP
40 West 20th Street, New York, NY 10011-4211, USA
10 Stamford Road, Oakleigh, Melbourne 3166, Australia

The Economic History Society 1991
Emigration from Europe 1815–1930 first published by
The Macmillan Press Limited 1991
First Cambridge University Press edition 1995

Printed in Great Britain at the University Press, Cambridge

A catalogue record for this book is available from the British Library

Library of Congress cataloguing in publication data

Baines, Dudley, 1939–
  Emigration from Europe, 1815–1930 / prepared for the Economic
History Society by Dudley Baines.
     p.   cm. – (New studies in economic and social history)
  Includes bibliographical references and index.
  ISBN 0 521 55270 2 (hardback). – ISBN 0 521 55783 6 (pbk.)
  1. Europe – Emigration and immigration – History. I. Economic
History Society. II. Title. III. Series.
  JV7590.B35   1995
  304.8'094'09034–dc20   95–18245
                                                             CIP

ISBN 0 521 55270 2 hardback
ISBN 0 521 55783 6 paperback

CE

Contents

1
Problems in the history of European emigration, 1815–1930

The movement of large numbers of people from Europe to the Americas and other parts of the world was one of the most important features of the international economy in the years after the Napoleonic wars. More than 50 million people were directly involved. Emigration could not fail to have profound effects on both the sending and the receiving countries.

There are some ambiguities in both the emigration and immigration statistics of individual countries but they are not important enough to obscure the main features of the movement. The temporal pattern was that the volume and the rate of emigration rose to the First World War, continued at a lower rate in the 1920s, and collapsed in the international depression of the early 1930s. There were large fluctuations around the upward trend, however. Emigration rates peaked in 1854, 1873, 1883, 1907 and 1913. The geographical pattern was that, in general, European emigration spread from west to east. In the early nineteenth century, most emigrants came from Britain and Ireland. By the 1850s, emigration had become important from some of the German States and Scandinavia. By the early twentieth century, emigration from Norway, Sweden, Germany, Ireland and Switzerland had passed its peak. But very large numbers of emigrants were leaving from Italy and from many parts of southern and eastern Europe (Ferenczi and Willcox, 1929–31, I, *236–88*).

About 52 million people were recorded as having left European countries for overseas destinations between 1815 and 1930. Rather more were recorded as having arrived. It is thought that the true number of emigrants was closer to 60 million. The reason for the discrepancy is that 'emigrant' and 'immigrant' were often rather

Table 1 *Recorded immigration (passenger arrivals) in the main immigration countries, 1815–1930*

	Millions
United States	
(from Europe)	32.6
(from the Americas)	4.7
Canada	4.7 (7.2)*
Australia	3.5
Brazil	4.3
Argentina	6.4
Total immigration from Europe	54.0

*At least 2.5 million subsequently moved from Canada to the USA. These numbers include people who, strictly speaking, were not immigrants.
Ferenczi and Willcox, 1929–31, I, *230–1*; Mitchell, 1983, *139–47*.

loosely defined. They could, for example, include people who were really visitors or on business.

The United States was by far the most important destination with some 33 million immigrants between 1815 and 1930. The other main destinations were Argentina, Canada, Brazil and Australia. Argentina had about 6 million immigrants, Canada at least 5 million, Brazil about 4 million and Australia about 3.5 million (Table 1).

About 11 million of the 52 million recorded emigrants came from Britain, 10 million from Italy, 7 million from Ireland, nearly 5 million from Germany or its component states, and over 5.5 million from Spain and Portugal. Less than a quarter of the emigrants came from the rest of Europe – Russia, eastern Europe, the Low Countries, France and Scandinavia (Table 2).

There was considerable variance in the average rate of emigration from the individual European countries. For example, Norway lost an average of two people out of every 300 in each year 1861–1910. France lost one person in every 5000. Table 3 shows the relative incidence of emigration. The countries most affected were Ireland, Norway, Scotland, Italy, England, Sweden, Portugal and Spain. These data can be misleading, however. In the first

Table 2 *Recorded emigration from European countries, 1815–1930 (1914 boundaries)*

	Millions
Britain	11.4
Italy	9.9
Ireland	7.3
Austria-Hungary	5.0
Germany*	4.8
Spain	4.4
Russia[†]	3.1
Portugal	1.8
Sweden	1.2
Norway	0.8
Finland	0.4
France	0.4
Denmark	0.4
Switzerland	0.3
Netherlands	0.2
Belgium	0.2
Europe	51.7

* Includes Prussian Poland.
[†] Includes Russian Poland.
Ferenczi and Willcox, 1929–31, I, *230–1*; Mitchell, 1980, *146–58*.

place, emigration from some of the southern and eastern European countries was important only towards the end of the period and was seriously curtailed by the introduction of restrictions after the First World War. Most important, some countries (notably Germany and Austria-Hungary) were very large and heterogeneous. In general, when emigration rates from the individual 'provinces', 'counties' or 'states' of the European countries can be calculated, we find that some regions within the European countries produced relatively large numbers of emigrants and other regions produced relatively few. The variance in regional emigration rates suggests that the country may not be the appropriate unit of analysis.

The most important characteristic of European emigration was diversity. There were emigrants from every European country who

Table 3 *Overseas emigration. European countries (1914 boundaries), 1851–1930*

	Annual average rate per 1000 population				
	1851–60	1861–70	1871–80	1881–90	1891–1900
Ireland	14.0	14.6	6.6	14.2	8.9
Norway	2.4	5.8	4.7	9.5	4.5
Scotland	5.0	4.6	4.7	7.1	4.4
Italy			1.1	3.4	5.0
England	2.6	2.8	4.0	5.6	3.6
Sweden	0.5	3.1	2.4	7.0	4.1
Portugal		1.9	2.9	3.8	5.1
Spain				3.6	4.4
Denmark			2.1	3.9	2.2
Finland				1.3	2.3
Austria-Hungary			0.3	1.1	1.6
Switzerland			1.3	3.2	1.4
Germany			1.5	2.9	1.0
Netherlands	0.5	0.6	0.5	1.2	0.5
Belgium				0.9	0.4
France	0.1	0.2	0.2	0.3	0.1

	1901–10	(1913)	1921–30
Ireland	7.0	6.8	5.9
Norway	8.3	4.2	3.1
Scotland	9.9	14.4	9.2
Italy	10.8	16.3	3.4
England	5.5	7.6	2.7
Sweden	4.2	3.1	1.8
Portugal	5.7	13.0	3.2
Spain	5.7	10.5	6.3
Denmark	2.8	3.2	1.7
Finland	5.5	6.4	2.1
Austria-Hungary	4.8	6.1	1.4
Switzerland	1.4	1.7	1.4
Germany	0.5	0.4	1.0
Netherlands	0.5	0.4	0.5
Belgium	0.6	1.0	0.3
France	0.1	0.2	

Adapted from Ferenczi and Willcox, 1929–31, I, *200–1* and Mitchell, 1980, *150–3*.

went to a wide range of destinations. They included people from every occupation and social class. Some emigrants were escaping famine or pogrom but some were rich. On arrival, a few became 'pioneers' and moved into unsettled territory. More took up farms in areas that were already settled. Even more took urban jobs. Some of the emigrants returned to Europe as failures but, as we shall see, many more of those who returned had always intended to return home. We must also remember that in most countries, internal migration affected more people than emigration. And in some countries 'emigration' could mean a move to another country within Europe.

The phenomenon of European emigration was not confined to the nineteenth and early twentieth centuries. Emigration was well established from Britain and Ireland in the seventeenth century, for example. Nor was it a uniquely European phenomenon. Migration from Russia into Siberia is thought to have involved 10 million people between 1815 and 1914 (Hoerder, 1985, *10*). India, China and Japan were also important sources of emigrants in this period. We must remember, too, that the enforced emigration of blacks to the Americas was numerically more important than white emigration until the third decade of the nineteenth century. About 8,000,000 blacks had entered the Americas before 1820 compared with fewer than 2,500,000 whites (Eltis, 1983, *28*).

How can we make sense out of this diversity? One way is to consider emigration as part of the development of an international economy (e.g. Hansen, 1940; Taylor, 1971). We know that the industrialisation of Europe led to an increase in the interdependence of Europe and some of the overseas countries. Industrialisation affected transport and communications, the availability of European capital for overseas investment and the growth of markets in Europe for overseas products (see Foreman-Peck, 1983, *102–6, 144–52*; Kenwood and Lougheed, 1983, *133–43*). In the international economy model, the direction of migration flows is determined by the relative availability of factors of production. In general, the European countries in the nineteenth century had an abundant supply of capital and labour relative to the available resources (widely defined) but there were overseas countries where resources were scarce relative to capital and labour. At the margin, investment was likely to be more profitable in these countries and incomes higher than in Europe. This led to a redistribution of the European population. Only 4 per cent of ethnic Europeans were living outside Europe and Siberia around 1800. By the First World War this proportion was 21 per cent and rising.

The 'international economy' model could be viewed in a different way, however. We can call this alternative view the 'core-periphery' model. The idea owes a great deal to studies of contemporary migration from the third world (e.g. Piore, 1979; Harris and Todaro, 1970). These studies suggest that emigration does not necessarily lead to the narrowing of income differentials between the origin and destination countries. Instead, it is argued, advanced capitalist development in the 'core' countries increases the demand for unskilled labour. The demand is often met by immigrants from the 'peripheral' countries. The labour market in the 'core' countries tends to be segmented and the immigrants find it difficult to improve their position. This is partly because of ignorance and prejudice. Many of the immigrants are 'target earners' or 'birds of passage', who return to the periphery where their earnings partially support other people. We should note that both the 'international economy' model and the 'core-periphery' model have political implications. Essentially, they are about the ability of capitalist development to increase welfare generally, or only partially.

The core-periphery model is a useful way of considering European emigration in the late nineteenth and early twentieth centuries. By that time, a high proportion of emigration – from the south and east of Europe – was temporary and was undertaken for the purpose of supplementing the family income. Some historians have described these emigrants as 'labour migrants' which distinguishes them from the 'settlers' who were predominant among the earlier emigrants from northern and western Europe. It is possible, however, that this distinction is too rigid. Not all southern and eastern European emigrants were temporary nor were all northern and western European emigrants 'settlers'. The key question is whether the emigrants *intended* to 'settle', to stay for a long period or to return quickly. This decision must have been profoundly affected by transport changes, for example.

Underlying both the international economy and the core-periphery models are judgements about the behaviour of individuals and the influence affecting the emigration decision. In effect, we start with an assumption that potential emigrants were in possession of sufficient information about one or more possible destinations. This is a large assumption, of course. We can then say that individuals calculated how high their lifetime welfare would be if they emigrated, and compared it to their expected lifetime welfare if they remained where they were. 'Welfare', in this sense, would include all benefits, both material and non-material. If the difference in their expected welfare was substantial, they could be expected to leave – assuming that the prospective emigrants were prepared to accept the degree of uncertainty and could afford the cost of passage, including the income that was forgone before they could take up employment.

Many historians have implicitly used this simple model. Various characteristics of the European and overseas countries, for example, 'population pressure', 'poverty', 'free land' are related to the growth and fluctuations in the emigration rate (e.g. Thomas, 1954).

We will discuss the idea of push-pull more fully below. One problem is that 'push' and 'pull' factors are not independent of each other. We can be fairly sure that potential emigrants weighed both the advantages and the disadvantages of moving to another country against the advantages and disadvantages of staying. In other words, the majority of emigrants – i.e. those who were not escaping from pogrom or famine – would have had great difficulty in explaining whether they had been 'pushed' out of Europe or 'pulled' towards their destination.

If the 'push-pull' formulation were applicable to European experience we would expect that emigration rates from individual European countries would be inversely related to their degree of economic development, or perhaps inversely related to their rate of economic development. And we would expect emigration rates to fall as European countries developed. Strictly, emigration rates would fall if the income differentials between the European and overseas countries narrowed. On the other hand, if emigration was largely a consequence of the increasing integration of the international economy, so that many of the uncertainties of emigration were reduced, we would expect that emigration rates would increase as countries became more developed.

We must be careful, however, about any explanation which depends on the characteristics of the environment from which the emigrants came or to which they were going. People chose to emigrate. It was a *selective* process and emigrants were rarely a random sample of the population from which they were drawn. The most frequent selection was by age. Most groups of emigrants contained more young adults and fewer children and old people than the home population. There was also selection by gender. In general, men were more likely to emigrate than women. But the emigrant sex ratio was not the same in every country. It could depend on whether the emigrants were likely to return, for example. Selection by occupation and income was also common but, again, occupational selection varied from one country to another. It is also possible that emigrants were selected psychologically. We will return to this point later.

We must not forget that economic growth was occurring in the European economies in the nineteenth century. In some cases, incomes were, on average, rising faster in the countries that were losing emigrants than in the countries that were gaining them. Does that mean that emigrants from countries with strong economic growth tended to be economically 'peripheral'? Would we expect that the emigrants came from the more remote areas or perhaps had followed occupations that were threatened? This would be the implication if emigration was determined by the 'push' and the 'pull'. As we have seen, it is possible to take a different view. The key to emigration may have been the availability of information. Information was important because it reduced uncertainty. And, of course, the development of economic relations between countries made it much easier to acquire the information that made emigration possible. In this case, we would expect that the emigrants would tend to come from places that were closer to the centre of economic change – perhaps from the capital city. Nor would there be any particular reason to expect that the emigrants were from redundant occupations.

Another aspect of emigrant selection is the question of 'deviance'. Did an emigrant tend to be an 'outsider' – someone who was rejecting some aspect of the society in which he or she was living? There are many examples of 'deviant' behaviour among those people who left for religious reasons, e.g. the Mormons

(Rundblom and Norman, 1976, *116–18*; Walker, 1964, *16–18, 78–80*; Taylor, 1965, *148–55*). Is it possible to go beyond these examples, however? Did people who chose to face the uncertainties of emigration always tend to be socially 'radical'? And did those who chose to stay behind tend to be socially 'conservative'? Or were emigrants 'radical' by definition? Unfortunately, this proposition is very difficult to test, not least because we do not have an objective definition of 'radical' or 'conservative'. Consider a place which produced large numbers of emigrants. In this case, would it be 'radical' to consider emigration and 'conservative' not to? For example, a letter arrives from Chicago encouraging someone to join the writer. The letter says that well paid jobs are currently available. It also contains money. A move to Chicago is obviously a step into the unknown. But in this scenario – which is not particularly extreme – how big is the step? And if the reason for going to Chicago is to earn money to maintain a 'traditional' lifestyle in Europe, as in the core-periphery model, would emigration be 'radical' behaviour?

This brings us back to our original question. In what sense can we think of all European emigration as part of a single, although complex, phenomenon? Should we expect to find similarities in the economies and societies of, for example, Britain, Norway, Ireland and Italy which had the highest emigration rates, that we would not find in France, the Netherlands and Switzerland, which had the lowest emigration rates? Or do we need a different explanation for the emigration from each country? Or should we look for similarities in the way that emigration occurred and the institutions which facilitated it, rather than in the characteristics of the places from which the emigrants came?

There is, however, a more important problem. We cannot know what actually passed through the minds of potential emigrants. We can be fairly sure that personal motives, often connected with particular stages in the life-cycle, played a large part in the decision to emigrate. And we can be fairly sure that there were psychological barriers to emigration that had to be overcome. Historians have been able to gain valuable insights into the motives of individual emigrants. The letters that passed between the emigrants and their original home have been the most important source (Erickson, 1972; Thomas and Znaniecki, 1918/1984). But we face a difficult problem here. Our knowledge of the personal reasons that must have affected the decision to emigrate relate only to a minute proportion of European emigrants. On the other hand, there is a large body of evidence about economic and social conditions in the areas from which the emigrants came or, in some cases, the economic and social condition of the emigrants themselves. It is not surprising that research has tended to emphasise the economic and social causes of emigration – in so far as they can be identified. The same point can be made about the experience of emigration itself. Individual emigrants were facing a break with home, often a difficult journey and an uncertain future. Emigration may have been the most important single experience that many of them would face. But it is an experience about which we have little direct evidence.

2

Sources of historical information

All European countries published statistics on annual outward movement. They are summarised in Ferenczi and Willcox (1929–31, I, *236–88*). These data were usually compiled from counts of passenger sailings, or from the issue of emigration passports (Finland, Italy, Hungary in some years), or from the contracts made between ships' masters and the emigrants (Denmark, Sweden). In addition, all the destination countries recorded annual inward movement. We must use these data with some caution, as can be seen when we compare departures and arrivals. Overseas arrivals appear to have exceeded European departures by some 10 million. In the early years, the recording of outward movement was inefficient in some European countries. There was also some clandestine emigration – commonly to avoid military service. One place where we would expect to find clandestine emigration was where ethnic minorities were liable to military service in an 'alien' army.

The greatest source of difficulty is that European countries were much less likely to record the annual number of arrivals, and destination countries were less likely to record departures. This is a problem because return migration became common. By the early twentieth century most countries had a return migration rate exceeding a quarter of outward movement and some countries had much higher return migration rates (Gould, 1979, *609*). Consequently, we may not know if an increase in emigration that we are observing was partly countervailed by an increase in returns. This raises some important conceptual issues which we will discuss below.

We can, of course, estimate the effect of total net migration (emigration less immigration) out of a country. This must be the difference between the total population recorded in one census and the next, plus births, minus deaths in the intervening period.

i.e. net emig. $(1-2) = $ pop $(2) -$ [pop.(1) + births $(1-2)$
$-$ deaths $(1-2)$]

This calculation tells us about the relative importance of migration compared with the other components of population growth but only accurately within an inter-censual period. The measure also includes the effect of migration to and from other European countries or, in the case of the United States, immigration from Canada and Mexico, which was very high in some years. Italy provides a good example of the difficulties: 13,400,000 were recorded as having left Italy between 1881 and 1911, of which something over a half went overseas. But the net population loss was only 3,800,000 (Di Comite, 1986, *153*).

In recent years, historians have begun to analyse some of the original returns from which the published data were compiled. The listings of the passengers on emigrant ships have proved to be the most useful source. The analysis of the ships' lists and similar materials is arduous and time-consuming but in some cases it is possible to show the age, occupation and marital condition of individual emigrants and the name of the community which they had just left. Scandinavian lists are often of high quality and historians have been able to build up a comprehensive picture of the economic and social condition of Swedish, Norwegian and Danish emigrants (Hvidt, 1975; Rundblom and Norman, 1976; Norman and Rundblom, 1988; Semmingsen, 1960, 1972). Most of the United States lists of immigrants have also survived and some have been used to analyse British immigration (Erickson, 1972, 1986, 1989). Australian and New Zealand lists also exist. Unfortunately, there are no equivalent data during most of the nineteenth century for Britain nor for most countries in southern and eastern Europe and Latin America. We know more about the million or so Swedish emigrants than we do about the 11 million British.

It has been possible in some cases to trace names from the ships' lists in other nominal listings, for example, the manuscript census in the destination countries. Identification of the immigrants would then depend on their degree of geographical concentration. One study was able to trace a third of all Dutch immigrants to the United States between 1835 and 1870. (Total immigration was only 15,000 families, however (Swierenga, 1986, *118–19*).) On the other hand, it is very difficult to locate British immigrants in the United States in any numbers because, unlike the Dutch, they were dispersed across the whole country.

To return to a previous point, information about the social and economic characteristics of emigrants can tell us about their motivation only by inference. If we have very sensitive data, we may be able to discover that emigrants were poorer than those who did not emigrate. What we do not know is what the emigrants thought about their prospects.

The most direct evidence about motivation is contained in the letters sent by emigrants, usually to their relations. There are several important collections of these letters but unfortunately, the number of surviving letters is tiny when compared with a total of more than 50 million emigrants. It is also likely that the letter-writers were a biased sample of emigrants. For example, emigrants who wrote home may have been people who found it difficult to settle in their new country. Or they may have been anxious to persuade others to follow (Erickson, 1972, *13–21*).

Before the 1960s, most studies of migration were written from the point of view of the receiving countries. The main interest was to explain how well the immigrants had adapted to their new home, their degree of social and economic mobility and the extent to which they had maintained their old culture or had been 'assimilated' into the host culture. 'Assimilation' was considered usual. Another interest of the early literature was 'filiopietism' – to highlight the contribution of 'Italian-Americans' or 'Swedish-Americans' to the host country. The causes of the original move were often taken for granted. It was usually enough to point to the problems in agriculture, the existence of population pressure and the decline of rural industries in Europe. Once the links with the overseas countries were created it was self-evident to these historians that many of the 'huddled masses' would want to 'escape'.

The vocabulary of early historians is very interesting. An 'emigrant' tended to mean someone who was lost to the 'homeland'. An 'immigrant' was someone who had rejected his or her 'homeland' for a new (and superior) environment. He or she was 'uprooted' – to quote from the title of a well-known book of the 1950s (Handlin, 1951). It was possible that the 'immigrants' carried European attitudes and 'culture' with them but the essence of emigration was normally seen as the break between Europe and an overseas country.

More recently, research on European emigration has changed in several ways. Firstly, the ability of the computer to analyse large data sets has allowed historians to address a large number of new detailed questions. These questions have been more likely to put the emigrant and the emigration decision at the centre of the story. Historians have become much more concerned with the links between Europe and the countries to which the emigrants went, and how those links affected the scale and character of the emigration. Another concern is how these links affected the immigrants after they arrived (e.g. Glazier and De Rosa, 1986; Erickson, 1980; Gjerde, 1985; Hoerder, 1985; Gould, 1979; Hvidt, 1975; Kero, 1974; Ostergren, 1987; Rundblom and Norman, 1976).

3
Emigration and economic change in Europe

The peaks and troughs of emigration from the different European countries tended to coincide. This is particularly interesting. There were great differences in the economies and the societies of European countries. Is it likely, therefore, that the timing of emigration was determined by changes in economic and social conditions within the individual European countries? It is surely more probable that the timing was mainly determined by the degree of prosperity (e.g. the availability of jobs) in the destination countries.

This conclusion concerns the timing of emigration. It does not mean that fluctuations in the prosperity of the destination countries determined the *rate* of emigration from Europe. The decision to emigrate had two components: whether to go and when to go. The former was the more important. It was a complicated and difficult decision. But once the decision to emigrate (or to consider emigration) was made, it was not unreasonable for intending emigrants to wait until the prospects of employment and wage levels were favourable. The implication is that potential emigrants had some accurate knowledge about economic opportunities in the places to which they were going. This is an important point for which there is a great deal of independent evidence.

Conditions in many European countries in the nineteenth century were consistent with a high rate of emigration. For example, falling mortality led to faster population growth in most countries. Western European countries were the first affected, but by the 1880s, population was growing at the unprecedented level of more than 1 per cent per annum in most of eastern Europe as well.

Emigration spread from western to eastern Europe at much the same time. The main exception was France which had low population growth. But France also had very low emigration. In extreme cases emigration was related to famine, as in southern Germany and Ireland in the 1840s. But famine may not have been a sufficient cause of emigration. Obviously, people who were most affected by a famine may have been too poor to emigrate, or possibly they may not have had contacts in the outside world. In other words, the idea of 'crisis' emigration may be simplistic.

Recent work on a number of historical famines has begun to question the cause of the deaths, and by implication, the effect of famine on emigration. The suggestion is that deaths were more likely to be caused because some people could not acquire food even when there was no absolute food shortage. The problem was not the amount of food but how it was distributed (Sen, 1981, *45–51, 75–83*). The Irish famine of 1846–8, which was the most important in the history of European emigration, may be a case in point. Many writers have argued that the Irish famine was avoidable and that much of the blame should be laid at the door of the British government (Fitzpatrick, 1984, *27–9*; Mokyr, 1983, *52–64, 279–94*; Ó Gráda, 1989, *61–2*). This view has recently been severely criticised by Solar, who showed that crop destruction in Ireland was much more serious than in any other famine in nineteenth-century Europe. He also argued that the famine had a long-term effect on Irish agriculture, and hence, on Irish emigration – a point to which we will return (Solar, 1989, *116, 123–8*; Mokyr, 1983, *34–8*).

The effect of pogroms on Jewish emigration in the late nineteenth and early twentieth centuries has also been subject to scrutiny. Russian-Jewish emigration did rise in times of persecution, and particularly during the Kishinev pogroms of 1903. Even so, Jewish emigrants seem to have been highly selected: they included relatively large numbers of skilled handicraft workers, exactly the sort of people whose skills were easy to transfer. We also know that there was heavy Jewish emigration from Austria-Hungary in the same period. (Jewish emigration rates from Austria-Hungary were two-thirds those from Russia.) But Jews had nearly full civil rights in Austria-Hungary. In other words, political discrimination can have been only one cause of Jewish emigration (Kuznets, 1975, *87–8, 105*).

After the middle of the nineteenth century, there were few serious famines in Europe. But since the amount of agricultural land was essentially fixed, population growth was bound to affect rural society, and in turn it could affect emigration. In some parts of Europe, agricultural holdings were subdivided so that it became more difficult to keep a family on a single holding. Subdivision occurred in parts of Ireland, Polish Galicia, northern Portugal, southern Germany and Italy, for example (Zubrzycki, 1953, *253–5*; Norman and Rundblom, 1988, *39–42*; Walker, 1964, *47–8*; Brettell, 1986, *113*).

Emigration from some countries has also been linked to the increased commercialisation of agriculture. The growth of urban markets tended to increase the value of agricultural land which, in turn, increased the income of farmers. But some people either had no land or had only a tenuous hold on it. These people needed access to land owned by the better-off farmers. But such land was increasingly taken for commercial agriculture. There are examples of this in parts of eastern Europe, and in Norway (Gjerde, 1985, *16–24, 37–9*). The increased concentration of landholdings could also be the result of political changes as when many peasants were dispossessed of land in the Polish Provinces and in Hungary after 1848. Some peasants were replaced by migrant workers. By the late nineteenth century these eastern European countries had a 'rural proletariat of nearly 5 million people (Bade, 1987, *67–8*; Morawska, 1985, *25*; Walker, 1964, *165–6*; Zubrzyski, 1953, *252*).

We can see that rural Europe was not inhabited by an homogeneous and immobile peasantry. There were, however, some common threads in the complex set of changes that were affecting rural Europe. One was that it became more important for those with little or no land to acquire cash. This could be acquired in several ways including harvest migration, the manufacture of industrial products in the home or local workshops, or temporary migration to the urban areas. Industrial products were an important source of family income in many rural areas. Textiles were the most important. But this income could be threatened by the growth of low-cost factory production in the urban areas. (Examples include the effect of the development of Manchester on

Ulster, of Lower Austria on rural Galicia or of the Ruhr on rural Westphalia (Collins, 1982, *204–6*; Kampheofner, 1986, *189*). We could make a general argument about the causes of emigration. Part of the European population became peripheral in the later nineteenth century because the economic development of Europe implied an increase in specialisation. Small proprietors and workers were faced with a choice between accepting a fall in their standard of living, finding alternative employment, which may not have been possible, or migration. We could expect that most of the 'peripheral' emigrants came from agriculture. But in the industrial countries we would also expect to find industrial workers with redundant skills among the emigrants. This seems to have been the case among early nineteenth-century British emigrants, for example (Erickson, 1980, 1989).

The changes in the European economies could not of themselves lead to an increase in emigration. There had to be a means of escape. That escape was provided by the development of the 'regions of recent settlement' (the United States, Canada, Australia, New Zealand, South Africa, Argentina, Uruguay and Brazil). These countries were distinguished by a large supply of natural resources relative to the supply of labour and capital. In the nineteenth century there was a striking fall in transport costs from Europe to these countries and from the coasts of these countries to the interior. This made it profitable for both labour and capital to move to them (Kenwood and Lougheed, 1983, *146–7*; Foreman-Peck, 1983, *102–6*). The extreme case of emigrants moving towards a resource-rich country was the gold rushes, for example to California in 1849 and to Victoria in 1851. Goldfield migration was not a large proportion of European emigration, however.

Until the later nineteenth century the majority of immigrants into the regions of recent settlement entered agriculture (Irish emigrants were a notable exception). But there was a limit to the size of the agricultural labour force. Agriculture in these countries was mainly conducted on an extensive scale, both where the family farm was dominant, as in the United States, or where there was relatively little opportunity for the small farmer, as in Australia and Argentina. By the early twentieth century the only country that still had an open frontier was Canada. The United States had become the most important industrial country in the world. And all the regions of recent settlement were becoming highly urbanised because of the growth of transport facilities, urban services and even a little manufacturing. (These changes were related to the high productivity of agriculture, of course.) The upshot was that, from the later nineteenth century, more opportunities were being created for European immigrants in the urban areas of these countries than had been possible in agriculture.

The development of the regions of recent settlement also allowed cheaper food and agricultural raw materials to enter the European market. This could have serious effects on rural society, for example in Italy where there was an agricultural crisis in the 1880s and 1890s. But the effect of cheap agricultural imports varied from one European country to another. The response in Germany, France and Sweden was the introduction of tariffs. In Britain, the Netherlands, Denmark and Switzerland, cheap imported grain was used as an input for the livestock and dairying industry. And, of course, some European countries, such as Hungary and Russia, were grain exporters. In other words, cheap food imports did not increase the pressures on rural society in every country. But when they did, we might expect emigration to rise.

It would be difficult to deny that the rate of emigration from European countries owed something to the effects of population growth, changes in rural society and the development of an international economy. But creating a list of factors that are likely to have affected the decision to emigrate does not get us very far. Put another way, it is hardly surprising that the majority of European emigrants were poor or came from rural areas since these were the characteristics of a high proportion of the European population. We need to know if the rural poor were over- or under-represented among the emigrants, or whether the degree of population pressure, the changes in rural society and the extent of exposure to the international economy would reasonably predict the differences in emigration rates from the European countries. Most important, we need an explanation of why relatively few emigrants left Europe compared with the large number of people who must have been affected by the forces of change.

But emigration was not the only solution to the problems of

European rural society. In Italy, for example, there were relatively few emigrants from the regions where agriculture was dominated by large estates which were worked by labourers or share farmers (i.e. *latifundi*). In the main, rural Italian emigrants came from regions which had small or medium farms. An explanation for this pattern is that many of the Italian emigrants went in order to obtain cash with which to purchase land. Where the small man could not purchase land there was little emigration. On the other hand, these areas were characterised by relatively strong and militant agricultural trade unions. Emigration and militancy seem to have been substitutes for each other (Macdonald, 1963, 65–74).

There are a large number of quantitative studies on European emigration. They are largely concerned with emigration from northern and western Europe (Britain, Sweden, Norway and Denmark) to the United States and occasionally to Australia. The concentration on northern and western Europe is unfortunate, since we cannot test whether emigration from southern and eastern Europe was governed by different factors, which is an important issue in the literature. This is not the place to review the quantitative studies in detail. There are several critical reviews (e.g. Gould, 1979; Neal, 1976; Williamson, 1974), and our remarks will be confined to general rather than technical issues.

The commonest specification has been to take the annual rate of emigration as the dependent (left-hand side) variable, and a series of variables designed to capture the economic and social conditions in the receiving and sending countries as the independent (right-hand side) variables. These variables are designed to capture the actual influences that affected the decision to emigrate. We can ask, therefore, whether they are a reasonable approximation of the factors that affected the decision?

Some of the models explain the variance in emigration rates over time quite well. But one problem has been the ability of different models to obtain different but statistically significant results about the same group of emigrants. The disagreement could be for several reasons, including model identification (the selection of appropriate data) and model specification (the selection of the precise hypothesis to be tested). An example would be the way that the models treat labour market conditions as a cause of emigration.

It turns out that differences in wage rates between the two countries (in so far as they can be measured) do not predict emigration very well. This is intuitively reasonable because we cannot expect the bulk of the emigrants to have known about changes in wage rates in an overseas country in great detail. It is more likely that potential emigrants would respond to changes in the availability of jobs – i.e. to the number of vacancies in the destination countries. Unfortunately, data on the availability of jobs and unemployment are much more suspect than data about wages. Hence, we might expect that when these variables are able to predict emigration the correlation is spurious (Neal, 1976, *262*). Another difficulty is internal migration. By the late nineteenth century, most European countries had at least one region, which was often the capital city, that was a major migrant destination. The emigration decision may have been affected by an alternative destination. Unfortunately, there are rarely adequate data to include an internal migration variable in the models.

There is also a difficulty with the dependent (left-hand side) variable. The models are trying to estimate the effect of changes in economic and social conditions on the flow of 'emigrants' between two countries. (We may be forced to substitute data about 'passengers' for data about 'emigrants'.) The emigration flow was composed of outward and return emigrants. As we will see, the rate of return migration could be extremely high. It also varied relatively to the rate of outward migration. Hence, the net flow of emigrants would be the more appropriate variable. Unfortunately, the annual rate of return is not always known and even when it is, has often been ignored. We should also note that the independent variables tend to relate to aspects of the labour market in the two countries. In this case, to use outward movement of all 'emigrants' as the dependent variable, which is the most common formulation, is inappropriate. It should include only prospective workers.

We cannot expect the models to tell us whether the emigrants were 'pushed' by conditions in Europe, or 'pulled' by conditions overseas. This is not an appropriate question, and not one that the emigrants themselves could have answered, had they been asked. The attraction of another country only has meaning when compared with conditions at home.

Those readers who are not of a quantitative disposition may be unimpressed by the problems of analysing emigration quantitatively. But we must remember what the great majority of the models are attempting to test: whether the rate of emigration from one country to another was determined by differences in the economic and social conditions in the two countries. If we are unable to model this relationship it implies that the emigration decision was not as simple as we first thought. In other words, if the determinist framework is inappropriate, then it is inappropriate for qualitative studies as well.

The usefulness, or otherwise, of the determinist model is clearer if we define the decision to emigrate very carefully. For example, once the decision to emigrate or not to emigrate had been made it was rational for the emigrants to delay their departure until a moment when, to take one example, they had a good chance of obtaining employment. If departure could be delayed until a more favourable time it would mean that the emigrants were in possession of adequate knowledge. The partial success of the models in predicting annual fluctuations in emigration shows that this must have been the case.

What the deterministic models do not tell us is why some people chose to emigrate and others chose not to. In one sense the more important question is not what factors caused people to emigrate but what caused so few people to emigrate. Obviously, 50 million people or so is a very large number, but as a proportion of the whole European population it is only 3 per 1000 per year. Furthermore, despite continuous immigration, wide differences in income levels in the destination countries and in Europe remained. In 1914, recent immigrants to the United States, Argentina or Australia could usually earn substantially more than in Europe. This means that more than 50 million could have benefited from emigration. Unfortunately, there are innumerable explanations why emigration was not greater than it was. Some of the European population may have known little or nothing about the overseas countries. Even when people were aware of the advantages of emigration they may have been too poor to undertake it. Equally, the objection to emigration may have been cultural. They may have been unwilling to change their lifestyles.

One way to try and find answers to these questions is to compare one region with another, or one group of migrants with another; in the jargon, by using cross-section rather than time-series analysis. There have been attempts to do this quantitatively for European countries but the emigration rates from different European countries do not seem to be systematically determined by the economic and social characteristics of these countries. The most likely reason for this result is that the nation state may not be the appropriate unit of analysis. The incidence of emigration was not evenly spread across the European countries but was very much higher from some areas (i.e. 'provinces' or 'counties') than from others. If we choose to study, say, Swedish emigration we ought to study the economic and social conditions in those areas from which the emigrants came, and the economic and social conditions in those areas from which few emigrants came, not conditions in Sweden as a whole.

How far was the development of the international economy an independent cause of European emigration? We could say that many emigrants moved from the periphery to one of the centres of the international economy, for example. Sometimes this was because the development of the centres had deleterious effects on the periphery. On the other hand the connection with the centres could be beneficial. In either case, migrants moved towards the richer parts of the international economy. The precise effect of the development of the international economy on the rate of emigration from any one place turns on the degree of integration. The integration of the international economy increased the rate of information exchange. Obviously, all emigration depended on a minimum of information. But quality information about the availability of jobs, for example, would reduce the uncertainties of emigration.

This point can be made another way. We do not have an objective definition of migration. We do not know whether moving from say, Brittany to Paris in the eighteenth century was a more difficult undertaking, in the sense that it involved more personal cost, than moving from Sicily to Chicago in the early twentieth century. Or from Cambridge, England, to Cambridge, Mass., a little later. There is no reason to expect that people with the most 'cause' to emigrate would be able to do so at the lowest 'cost'. The spread of quality information simply made emigration much easier. There is, however, a possibility of a circular argument here. Continued emigration from one place, for whatever cause, would itself increase contacts, in the shape of letters and returned migrants, between two communities. Hence, emigration explains emigration.

If there was an international labour market it is likely that it was very segmented. For example, in the early twentieth century Italian emigrants went to several destinations, including other European countries, the United States, Argentina and Brazil. The majority of this emigration was temporary. Virtually all of the emigrants who went to Europe returned, as did about half of those who went overseas (Gould, 1980a, *86*). If an international labour market was developing, we would expect that emigrants would move mainly in the direction of the highest income. This would imply that the majority of Italians, including the temporary emigrants, would go to the United States. But the majority of Italian emigrants always went to Europe and the United States rarely took more than two-thirds of the overseas emigrants (Di Comite, 1986, *153*). The pattern may have been because each emigrant knew of only one destination but this seems unlikely to have been generally true. Emigration was heavy from the Venezia and Lombardy to Brazil and from Piedmont and Lombardy to Argentina, i.e. from the same areas as were providing the emigrants to Europe (Gould, 1980a, *93*). The southern Italians also went to a range of destinations although, for them, the United States was the most important. Polish migration patterns in the early twentieth century were equally complex. Polish emigration rates were also high in the early twentieth century: 8 per cent of the Polish population left the country each year. Migration was in three main directions: to the United States, to cities in eastern Europe and to western Germany (Morowska, 1985, *28*).

The history of the great European ports also suggests that the international labour market was segmented. If the development of the international economy were a sufficient cause of emigration we would expect that the earliest emigrants came from the areas adjacent to the ports. But emigration rates from, for example, the environs of Rotterdam, La Rochelle or Hamburg were low. These cities were important emigration ports for people from other countries, i.e. Switzerland, southern Germany and the interior of Sweden (Norman and Rundblom, 1988, *114–16*).

Of course, there is no particular reason for nineteenth-century migration to conform to any expected pattern. The Italians who went to France or Argentina rather than to the United States, for example, could have come from particular villages, or possessed different skills or had different objectives. It is possible for the historian to explain all the exceptions to an 'expected' behaviour pattern. The problem is that there are a very large number of exceptions. There is no doubt that general models of migration can give us some very important insights. But these insights only take us so far. To know more about European migration we must disaggregate.

4

Emigration regions

It has been known for some time that there was great variation in the rate of emigration from the individual regions of the European countries. We do not have a comprehensive set of regional emigration rates from all European countries but some of the well-known emigration regions are listed in Table 4. We can see that about one-third of all Finnish emigrants came from one province (the area around Vaasa), about a half of all Austro-Hungarian emigrants in 1881–1910 came from Galicia and the Bukovina, about a quarter of all German emigration in the peak years came from West Prussia and Pomerania, and about 14 per cent of all English and Welsh emigrants in 1861–1900 came from the five counties of the West of England (Baines, 1986, *144, 158*; Chmelar, 1973, *319*; Foerster, 1919, *38*; Kero, 1974, *60*; Knodel, 1974, *109*).

Emigration regions raise the question of the most appropriate unit of analysis. This does not mean that the nation state in which he or she happened to be living was irrelevant to a potential emigrant. A minority of the European emigrants actually came from racial or ethnic minorities. These were often minorities with nationalist expectations and/or were suffering from degrees of discrimination. The Poles were heavily over-represented among emigrants from both Austria-Hungary and Germany. The bulk of the emigrants from Russia were from minorities (Jews, Poles, Lithuanians). Three-quarters of the Romanians entering the United States before the First World War were from the Transylvanian provinces of Hungary which were being Magyarised (Bobinska and Pilch, 1976, *13*; Ferenczi and Willcox, 1929–31, I, *416*; Kuznets, 1975, *50–1*).

There are some interesting paradoxes in regional emigration

Table 4 *Overseas emigration from some important regions (annual average per 1000 population)*

	Emigration	1000/p.a.
Italy (1901–13)	8,742,000	20
Arbruzzi	689,000	34
Basilicata	202,000	34
Calabria	614,000	37
Sicily	1,125,000	26
Austria (1881–1910)	1,799,000	2
Galicia	859,000	10
Finland (1860–1930)	360,000	2
S. Ostrobothnia	120,000	7
Germany (1871–95)	2,371,000	2
West Prussia	321,000	7
Pomerania	222,000	6
England & Wales (1861–1900)	2,349,000*	2*
West of England	323,000*	4*

* Net of returns.
Note that Italian overseas emigration was exceptionally high in the short period for which we have regional data.
Baines, 1986, *144*, *158*; Chmelar, 1973, *319*; Foerster, 1919, *38*; Kero, 1974, *60*; Knodel, 1974, *195*

rates. For example, the Italian regions of Calabria, the Arbruzzi and Sicily, had emigration rates eight to ten times higher than the regions of Emilia-Romagna and Sardinia which were equally poor. The question whether emigrants were more likely to have come from the poorest regions can only be answered by systematic quantitative analysis, of course. There have been only a few studies and the results have been mixed. Emigration from the individual Danish provinces, for example, does seem to have been negatively correlated with income (Hvidt, 1975, *38–40*). But a study of nineteenth-century Sweden could find no significant relationship between emigration rates from Swedish counties and their economic and social characteristics (Carlsson, 1976, *114–48*). Similarly, a study of English and Welsh counties in the late nineteenth century could find no relationship between their circumstances and their emigration rates (Baines, 1986, *166–77*). We should be a little careful of drawing general conclusions from English evidence, however. England was the most developed country in Europe and the English emigration experience in the late nineteenth century may have had little in common with rural Europe.

It is possible that we may not have the correct data with which to explain differential emigration rates. The 'province' or 'county' may not be the appropriate unit because there may have been areas of both high and low emigration within each province or county. The real emigration unit may have been the village. Alternatively, emigration may have been common in some families and rare in others. In either case, we need much more sensitive data before we can begin to explain the difference between a place of high emigration and one of low. Some Scandinavian countries do have better data and there are studies of emigration from individual localities. Interestingly, these studies have not been able to predict emigration rates simply from the economic and social circumstances of the localities (e.g. Rondhal, 1972, *273*; Tederbrand, 1972, *307*).

The most important characteristic of regional emigration to have been identified so far is continuity. Once emigration from a particular region was established it tended to remain high. The continuity of high emigration rates can be explained by a phenomenon called 'chain migration'. The idea behind chain migration is very simple. Emigration involved many uncertainties. There was uncertainty about the passage, the forward journey in the destination country and, probably most important, the prospects of employment. The prospect of setting up a farm, as many emigrants in the earlier nineteenth century wished to do, involved enormous uncertainty. It was usually safer to move from 'the known to the known'.

There are many examples of chain migration from both contemporary and historical populations. Consider the story of three Dalmatian brothers in the early twentieth century. One left Dalmatia in 1890 and worked in San Francisco, Sydney, Melbourne and Queensland. In 1906–7 he returned home, married a local woman and returned to Queensland. Another also left in 1890. He worked in Johannesburg, Adelaide, Sydney, the West Australian goldfields, Melbourne, New Zealand and Queensland. The third left in 1907 for Queensland. All the brothers arrived in Queensland at the same time (Price, 1963, *280–1*). This story contains an example of another phenomenon – 'stage' migration – which we will discuss later. Another of the many examples of chain migration concerns the village of San Giovanni Incario which lies in the mountains about halfway between Rome and Naples. When a study was made in the 1950s, the village, which then had 4000 inhabitants, was largely isolated from the rest of Italy. Very few outsiders had settled there. Yet there were 3000 natives of San Giovanni Incario living in the United States, divided between a suburb of Providence, Rhode Island, and a suburb of Boston, Massachusetts (Zimmerman, 1955).

Chain migration meant that immigrants tended to settle in a relatively limited number of locations. As late as 1910, 70 per cent of Norwegian immigrants in the USA were found in only six states: Wisconsin, Illinois, Iowa, Minnesota and the Dakotas (Norman and Rundblom, 1988, *146*). The small numbers of Dutch immigrants in the United States were even more concentrated: 56 per cent were living in only 18 of the 2300 counties in 1870 (Swierenga, 1986, *98*). Immigrants to the urban areas also tended to concentrate. In 1914, 370,000 of the 1,500,000 Italians in the USA were living in New York (Baily, 1983, *281*). Ethnic ghettos were largely a consequence of chains, some of which could be very narrow (Bodnar, 1985, *57–63*). In 1920, there were 200 families from the Sicilian town of Cinisi living at 6th St and Avenue A in New York (Baily, 1983, *291*). We should be careful here, however. Urban ghettos were neither mono-cultural nor all-pervasive (see below).

The number of emigrants moving in chains was large but it is difficult to tell precisely how large. For example, there have been several detailed and imaginative studies of the experience of immigrants in parts of the United States and, in particular, of the relationship between social change in Europe and changes within the new communities in the United States (e.g. Gjerde, 1985; Kamphoefner, 1987; Ostergren, 1987). These studies confirm the importance of chains. But it is only possible to answer questions of this detail and interest because there was a continuing relationship between the immigrant communities and the home communities. We can never know as much about the emigrants who did not move along chains. We may be in danger of overestimating the importance of chain migration.

And chains were not immutable. For example, emigration from northern Italy to Argentina in the late nineteenth century was characterised by strong chains (Baily, 1983, *290–2*). But in the early twentieth century two things happened: emigration from the northern regions began to shift towards the United States, and there was a very large increase in emigration from southern Italy, mainly to the United States. These patterns have important implications. The spread of emigration to new regions presumably means that new chains were being created. The fall in emigration from northern Italy to Argentina presumably means that some of the older chains must have been broken (Gould, 1980b, *284, 304*). The fact that some countries (notably Canada and Australia) found it necessary to subsidise immigration over long periods also shows the limitation of chains.

What happened as emigration spread to new regions within Europe? Did the original areas remain the most important, or was there a tendency for the incidence of emigration to even out between regions? In the Irish case the Famine seems to have spread emigration into new areas of the country. Before the 1840s, the heaviest emigration came from the northern and midland counties. In the Famine it spread to Connaught (which was in the west) and then to the whole of the west and south west. The fact that there was a cataclysmic famine makes Irish emigration a special case, of course (Fitzpatrick, 1984, *11–13*). But when we look at other countries, for example Italy, England and Wales and Hungary, we find that, over a period, the variance in regional emigration rates decreased (Baines, 1986, *285–98*; Gould, 1980b, *284*). This can only mean that information spread into new areas. We know that, in normal circumstances, there is no reason to expect that emigration started in the poorest regions and spread to the less poor. Therefore the question is, what did determine the diffusion of emigration?

It is possible that people in some areas were less responsive to the idea of emigration than people in others. When faced with a similar set of costs and benefits, some people were less willing to emigrate than others. In other words, the propensity of an individual to emigrate was affected by his or her culture. Since culture was created by what had happened in the past, we would expect that 'emigrators' and 'non-emigrators' would tend to be regionally concentrated. This could be the reason why the early religious emigrations from Germany (1816–17), Norway (1824) and Sweden (1830s) were not followed by significant numbers of emigrants for about 20 years (Gould, 1980b, *302*). Unfortunately, as we have said, there could be a hundred reasons why emigration did not occur. There is some work on England which is suggestive, however. Baines found that emigration from some of the most industrialised countries was relatively high in only one of the last four decades of the nineteenth century: the 1880s. It is unlikely that information about emigration prospects was scarce in these counties. Hence it seems that, on average, people in some countries were more likely to emigrate than people in other countries, even when the material benefits of emigration were the same for both groups. The reason for this differential behaviour is not known (Baines, 1986, *205–12*).

We have already noted that there were long-run fluctuations in the rate of emigration from the European countries. These fluctuations tended to follow the course of prosperity and depression in the countries to which the emigrants went. This implies that emigrants possessed information about economic and social conditions in the destination countries. But this does not necessarily mean that potential emigrants had long time horizons. It was more likely that the decision to emigrate simply responded to the situation in the overseas country at that particular time. Hence, if there was a succession of bad years, emigration could fall to very low levels. For example, there was effectively no net immigration into Australia for the ten years after 1893, when the economy was in relative decline compared with the expansion of the previous decade (Pope, 1981, *29*).

The marked long-run fluctuations in the rate of international migration are an important part of a debate concerning the dynamics of economic change, not least the question of whether the emigration caused the changes or the changes caused the emigration. The relation between fluctuations in emigration, the rate of growth and the direction of national and international investment will be examined below.

It is obvious that the first emigrants from a region cannot have travelled along paths that have been made by someone else. The emigrations from the German states in the 1830s and from Norway and Sweden in the 1850s were connected with Pietist religious movements which felt that they were under attack at home (Walker, 1964, *78–80, 112–14*; Norman and Rundblom, 1988, *53–61*). Some of the early religious emigrants, like the Mormons, were followed only by people with similar motivations (Hvidt, 1975, *148–55*). On the other hand, in parts of Germany, Sweden and Norway the religious emigrants probably created the chains that made it easier for people with different motivation to follow, although the chains may have taken some years to forge.

Potential emigrants seem to have obtained their information in two main ways: through letters from emigrants who had already gone and from the experience of emigrants who had returned to Europe. The number of letters sent to Europe is largely unknown. But in the case of Denmark, when the annual flow of letters is known, it increased faster than the rate of emigration (Hvidt, 1975, *187*; Norman and Rundblom, 1985, *53*). Individual letters have survived, of course. They were invariably concerned with family matters but often contained important details about job prospects, wages and so on (see the collections by Erickson and by Thomas and Znaniecki, for example). Of course, the information that the letters carried may have been biased. Their purpose could have been to encourage friends and relatives to join the writer of the letter. On the other hand, prospective emigrants often had access to letters from more than one emigrant. This was because of the existence of chains. In Ireland and Norway, for example, where there was a great deal of illiteracy, letters could even become public property to be read aloud by the village priest or pastor (Schrier, 1959, *41*; Semmingsen, 1978, *166*).

The flow of information to Europe can also tell us something about returned migrants. If the emigrants did rely to an extent on information that came from those who had returned, it follows that the majority of the returned migrants could not have been failures. If they had been, their experiences would presumably have tended to discourage, rather than encourage, emigration. There is little direct evidence about returned emigrants but the few studies (about Norway, Greece, Portugal and Italy) suggest that returned

migrants were no less prosperous than those who had not emigrated (Brettell, 1986, *113–14*; Cinel, 1982, *60*; Foerster, 1919,
454–5; Morawska, 1985, *65*; Saloutos, 1956, *117–31*; Semmingsen, 1960, *160*). The indirect evidence about returned emigrants is considerable, however. We know that emigration rates
and return migration rates were rising simultaneously in the early
twentieth century. This coincidence is difficult to reconcile if the
returned migrants had been failures. A more likely explanation is
that many of the emigrants had already decided to return before
they left Europe.

It is almost certain that of all the sources of information available
to prospective emigrants, returned migrants were the most valuable. (The Irish are an important exception. There was little return
migration to Ireland, as we will see.) In the early nineteenth
century, the effect of the first prosperous emigrants to return could
be remarkable, as in the case of the 'American fever' which swept
parts of Norway and Sweden in the 1850s and 1860s (Semmingsen, 1960, *30–1*). If the statement of one woman on her
return is to be believed, similar views were current in Hungary in
the early twentieth century. The United States was a country that
had 'thin bread with thick jam on it, and the land was flowing with
sausages, lager beer and chewing gum' (Curti and Burr, 1950,
219). In the long run, however, it was probably the more prosaic
knowledge obtained from the practical experience of the emigrants
that mattered. Unfortunately, one of the things that we do not
know is the proportion of the returned migrants who went back to
their original town or village. In the case of temporary emigrants
the proportion may have been high and we can only assume that a
large number of the longer-stay emigrants also returned home.
There is a Swedish study which shows that 80 per cent of the
emigrants from one province are known to have returned to their
native village, but this may be exceptional. (Incidentally, 50 per
cent of them re-emigrated (Tederbrand, 1972, *314*; 1985, *379*).)

Emigrants sometimes relied on newspapers from particular
destination cities rather than on letters. This seems to have
occurred in parts of Britain in the late nineteenth century
(Erickson, 1980, *327–8*). There is also an example where some
prospective Italian emigrants to Buenos Aires in the early twentieth
century are known to have taken the Buenos Aires newspapers

(Baily, 1983, *89*). These cases are probably exceptional but they raise a general point. If, in a particular case, impersonal sources of information were more important than letters and the experience of returned migrants, it implies that the labour market in the origin and destination regions was highly integrated. We know, for example, that some skilled London building workers were moving between London and New York and back again as early as the 1880s (Erickson, 1972, *359–64*). In other words, the building workers were effectively part of a single labour market that included London and New York.

5
Return migration

It is not always easy to count returned migrants but the best estimate is that more than a quarter of all emigrants in our period returned to Europe. The rate of return varied from one country to another, however. Over the whole period (1860–1930) about 20 per cent of Norwegians, Danes, Swedes and Finns returned and something under 40 per cent of the English and Welsh (1861–1913) (Baines, 1986, *135–8*; Hvidt, 1975, *187*; Tederbrand, 1985, *359*; Virtanen, 1985, *395*). In the early twentieth century, 30–40 per cent of northern Portuguese, Croats, Serbs, Hungarians and Poles were returning and 40–50 per cent of Italians (Brettell, 1986, *84*; Gould, 1980a, *609*; Krajlic, 1985, *406*; Palairet, 1979, *44–5*; Puskas, 1986, *233*). It is important to note that these data are adjusted to show the true rate of return. The true rate of return is lower than the rate of inward movement which is commonly given. The rate of inward movement simply relates all outward to all inward moves which overestimates the probability of an individual returning because it includes second-time emigrants and people who were not emigrants.

Return migration rates to most countries increased through the nineteenth century. But a higher proportion of southern and eastern European emigrants returned than northern and western European emigrants. The main reason for the increase in the rate of return to all countries was the improvement in transport. The reason that southern and eastern Europe had more return migration may have been because the bulk of the emigration occurred when transport was easier. Alternatively, emigration from southern and eastern Europe could have been fundamentally different in character. This has led to considerable debate which we will discuss later.

There were many reasons why emigrants returned, and it is not possible to make a rigid distinction between 'temporary' and 'permanent' emigrants. We cannot say, for example, that all those who returned in a short time were economic failures, since economic failure would in many cases make it difficult to return. In fact, it is possible that *most* emigrants expected ultimately to return. Scandinavian historians have said that if asked, virtually all the 2 million or more Scandinavian emigrants before 1914 would have said that they would eventually return to Europe. As we know, only 20 per cent did so. The same point has been made about Italian emigrants. Most Italian emigration was assumed to be temporary and Italians overseas talked of returning. Yet half of the overseas emigrants before 1914 did not return and settle in Italy (Cinel, 1982, *66*). The interesting question is why more people did not return.

In the middle of the nineteenth century there was a very good reason for not returning. The rigours of the journey were such that few chose to repeat it. A more important reason was that many prospered in a new country, acquired new habits and ways of thinking and, of course, established families. Even if they had originally expected ultimately to return, it became less attractive as time passed and, despite the increase in their wealth, less easy.

By the late nineteenth and early twentieth centuries, however, an increasing percentage of the emigrants had not only decided before they left Europe to return but had also decided to do so after only a few years. Stays of three and four years were common, which is about the shortest period it would take an unskilled worker to save enough to make the trip worthwhile (Palairet, 1979, *44–5*; Morawska, 1985, *70*). One reason for thinking that the emigrants *intended* to remain abroad for only a relatively short period is that many made a second emigration soon after returning. For example, 10 per cent of Italian immigrants into the United States in 1904 were entering for the second time, which suggests, incidentally, that their first move had not been a failure. There was usually a higher proportion of males among returned migrants than among emigrants (Livi-Bacci, 1961, *41*; Gould, 1980a, *55*). There is no reason why conditions in the overseas countries should have produced such a high ratio of men among returned migrants (eight to one among those who returned to Italy in some years).

Since the returned migrants cannot have changed sex in the overseas country, the male bias must have been selected in Europe. Hence, the men must have decided to return before they left. We cannot tell whether it was more common for temporary emigrants to aim to earn a sum of money or to stay for a target period. What is clear is that by the early twentieth century, the purpose of most temporary emigration was to make money that could be used in Europe, i.e. in southern and eastern Europe. Temporary emigration did occur from northern and western Europe in the later nineteenth and early twentieth centuries, notably from Britain, but it was never as important as from southern and eastern Europe. (Baines, 1986, *135–8*).

We have seen that remittances were an important feature of European emigration, and particularly remittances to southern and eastern Europe in the early twentieth century. One purpose was to supplement the incomes of relatives. Remittances could be critical in places where agricultural holdings were very small and where population was rising. Northern Portugal, for example, adopted partible inheritance in 1867. Average farm size declined. It became usual for a younger son to work overseas (80 per cent went to Brazil) until he could return with funds which could be used either for consumption or investment. The solution to population pressure was temporary, not permanent, emigration (Brettell, 1986, *70, 78*).

The Portuguese example shows that there is no necessary reason why emigration should change the home community. The experience of local emigrants would only be likely to lead to improvements in the local economy if changes were already occurring there or if the returned migrants had been working in an industry that was relevant to the local economy. Otherwise there would be no point of reference. Many Polish, Irish and southern Italian emigrants worked in industry. When they returned their experiences had little effect on agriculture in their home countries. It is also possible that temporary emigrants returned with only a limited experience of a different culture. They had often lived in dormitories or had boarded with people from similar backgrounds. This returns us to the general question of whether emigration was a 'radical' activity.

Remittances from emigrants were used to finance the emigration of other members of the family. It was quite common, for example, for a family member who had been sent overseas to send for additional members of the family. Livi-Bacci was able to show that the proportion of young male adults among Italian emigrants was at its highest when emigration from Italy was at a peak. As we have said, this was partly because much of the Italian emigration was temporary. But it is also consistent with young adult males being sent overseas when prospects were particularly favourable and sending for other family members at a later stage (Livi-Bacci, 1961, *41*).

Remittances could also be used by the emigrant himself. For example, an Italian might work for wages in the United States or Argentina in order that he or she might not have to work for wages in Italy. The family could be very important here. There were many people who could not emigrate without the support and blessing of their family, especially if a family farm was involved. Someone had to stay behind. But it is known that in some cases, in Italy, for example, the capital belonging to the returned migrant was for his exclusive use. However, in such a case he would probably have no claim on the family property (Bodnar, 1985, *183–97*).

The total value of remittances is not known with any certainty, nor do we know how the total was divided between different uses. We know the value of postal and money orders sent to some countries but the amount of cash that was carried by returned emigrants or placed inside letters is unknown. But the total was certainly large. For example, if the remittances had all been used to finance emigration, they would have been sufficient to pay for all of it. According to an important Congressional enquiry – the Dillingham Commission – about a third of those entering the United States in 1908–14 travelled on tickets paid for by previous immigrants. Scandinavian studies support this: 30 per cent of Finnish (1891–1914), and about 40 per cent of Swedish (1880s) and Norwegians (1872–4) were travelling on pre-paid fares (Brattne, 1976, *276*; Kero, 1974, *177–8*). This brings us back to motivation. For example, someone who was known to have received a pre-paid ticket was being 'pushed' as well as 'pulled' overseas.

6

Did emigration change in character?

There were always relatively large numbers of young adults among the emigrants. For example, in all years between 1840 and 1930, 65–75 per cent of American immigrants were aged 15–40 (Ferenczi and Willcox, (1929–31), II, *114*). This is to be expected. Emigration involved an investment decision in which current income, which can be defined very widely, was forgone in the expectation of a higher income in the future. The younger the emigrant the greater the return over his or her lifetime. Emigration also tended to occur at particular stages of the life cycle, for example, when people married and/or left the parental home. This is one of the reasons why some historians have thought that the availability of land (the chance of obtaining a holding) was an important cause of emigration from agricultural areas. We have argued that it is unlikely to have been a sufficient cause.

There were, however, some important changes in the family status of the emigrants. In the earlier part of the nineteenth century the typical emigrants were a young family, often accompanied by children – although they may not necessarily have travelled together. There were roughly equal numbers of males and females. By the later nineteenth century the typical emigrants were young single adults and males outnumbered females by about two to one. For example, in 1866–70 (which were peak years) only a third of Norwegian emigrants were young men (15–30). By 1911–15, three-quarters of Norwegian emigrants were young men (Semmingsen, 1960, *53–4*). The main exceptions to the changing pattern were Irish and Swedish emigrants. There was always a relatively high proportion of females among the former and a higher proportion of males among the latter. Most of the earlier emigrants entered agricultural occupations (again the Irish were an exception) and relatively few returned home. They were settlers, or to use the Scandinavian term, 'folk' emigrants. The later, 'individual', emigrants were more likely to enter urban and industrial occupations. They were also much more likely to return home. In the main, the rate of return was positively correlated with the proportion of young adult males. In the early twentieth century, for example, Italian and Greek emigration was dominated by young males but Jewish emigration was dominated by families.

There are several explanations for the change from 'folk' to 'individual' emigration. The first is cost. The cost of emigration was high in the earlier part of the nineteenth century. The cheapest individual fare from Liverpool to New York in 1850 was about a month's income for a skilled worker or two months' income for an unskilled worker. Passage from a Norwegian or German port was about twice as expensive. In addition, the emigrant had to forgo income. A journey from, say, Halland in Sweden to northern Minnesota could take three months and cost three months' income.

In the early nineteenth century, the Atlantic passage (by sailing ship) was not only slow – it took between three and ten weeks – but also extremely uncomfortable and hazardous. Some writers have gone so far as to claim that mortality on emigrant sailing ships in the early nineteenth century exceeded that on slave ships in the later eighteenth century, but this is incorrect. Recent estimates are that about 1.5 per cent of the emigrants from European ports to New York between 1836 and 1853 died on board or immediately after arrival. From UK ports to Quebec between 1841 and 1855 the proportion was similar. The average passage was 44 and 45 days respectively. This compares with estimates of mortality on slave ships that range from 5 per cent to 17 per cent (Cohn, 1984, *294*; Baily, 1983, *270–1*). We can assume, however, that the rigours of the journey in the early nineteenth century were such that few emigrants chose to repeat it. Most of the early emigrants had little alternative but to 'settle'.

The situation changed from the middle of the nineteenth century. The introduction of steam shipping on the North Atlantic in the 1860s was only one of a continuous series of improvements in transport and communications, including the introduction of regularly timetabled departures and the creation of shipping lines that catered for the emigrant trade. The most famous shipping company was Cunard which entered the emigrant trade in 1840 (Hyde, 1975, *59*; Taylor, 1971, *145–66*). The majority of the emigrant shipping companies were British-owned. Most emigrants from Sweden and Finland, for example, had to travel via Hull and Liverpool before the creation of the Norwegian-Amerika (1913) and Swedish-America (1915) lines. The main port for emigration from Congress and Prussian Poland was Hamburg. Trieste was the main port for Ukrainians and Croats. Fiume (Rijeka) became important in 1903 when the Hungarian government, who controlled the port, encouraged Cunard to use it (Krajlic, 1985, *413*).

Other important improvements were the development of railways in both the origin and destination countries, the sale of through tickets to overseas destinations, and improvements in reception arrangements (Curti and Burr, 1950, *211*). In other words, the price of the ticket was only one of many things that the prospective emigrant had to consider, as quantitative studies have confirmed (Oden, 1972, *92–3*).

The changes substantially reduced the uncertainties of emigration. It is also likely that they changed the nature of the decision to emigrate. As transport improved, emigration became less final. This made it easier for people to take the decision. The changes also favoured a relatively new kind of emigrant – one who expected to return within a relatively short period.

A further reason for the shift from 'folk' to 'individual' emigration was that the structure of the economies of the main destination countries changed. At the end of the century, the only country where it was relatively easy to acquire a family farm was Canada. (In some countries, notably Australia and (arguably) Argentina it had never been easy to enter farming without a great deal of capital.) The Canadian West developed relatively late because people had been rather unwilling to take up farms there. One reason was that farming in the United States had been more attractive. People would not take family farms in Canada until it became difficult to do so in the United States. The second reason was that the Canadian prairies could not properly be settled until new farming techniques for the dry soils had been developed.

On the other hand, as opportunities in agriculture declined in most countries, there was a big increase in the demand for labour in the urban areas and in industry. In the United States, for example, there were twice as many foreign-born workers in manufacturing, trade and transport in 1900 as there were in agriculture.

There is an important question of interpretation here. Emigration from southern and eastern Europe was not important until the later nineteenth century. 'Individual' emigrants were important almost from the beginning, as was a high rate of return migration. There was virtually no 'folk' stage in emigration from southern and eastern Europe. The reason that few emigrants from this part of Europe 'settled' could have been because settlement had become much more difficult. Few could have become farmers, for example, even if they had wanted to. On the other hand, before the later nineteenth century, most northern European emigrants had little choice but to settle, and mainly in agriculture.

Some historians have argued, however, that the 'New' emigration (to use the contemporary term) had little in common with emigration from northern Europe. There was a long tradition of temporary emigration within southern and eastern Europe. And temporary emigration between southern and northern Europe was also occurring (Gould, 1980b, *99–100*). Temporary emigration to the Americas can simply be seen as the 'American option' (Cinel, 1982, *41*). The most famous example was probably the 20,000 *golondrinas*, or 'swallows', who were moving annually between Italy and the River Plate before the First World War (Gould, 1980b, *93–5*). The interesting question here, is why the Argentine farmers preferred Italians to Argentines when the former demanded higher wages.

The fact that temporary emigration was more important from southern than from northern Europe can be explained by the familiar 'centre-periphery' argument. Since northern Europe was closer to the 'centre' and southern Europe to the 'periphery', temporary emigration could never have been as important from the former. It is possible, however, that the extent to which the southerners 'settled' and the extent of temporary emigration among northerners have both been underestimated. We know that return migration to Italy from Argentina and the United States (1861–1914) was 47 per cent and 52 per cent of outward movement, respectively (Gould, 1980a, *296*). This means that at least half of

Italian emigrants 'settled', a low proportion by the standards of most northern European countries but not much less than the proportion of English and Welsh emigrants in the same period (Baines, 1986, *139–40*). Earlier in the nineteenth century, there was a great deal of temporary emigration from the northern and western European countries, for example harvest migrations between Scandinavia and Germany and Ireland and Britain (Foerster, 1919, *131–4*; Walker, 1964, *53–8*). In other words, there was a time when parts of the northern countries could be regarded as 'peripheral' to the more developed parts of the European economy.

There is also some evidence that the emigration of individuals rather than families was beginning in the middle of the nineteenth century, notably from Britain (Baines, 1986, *139–40*; Erickson, 1972, *363*). This implies that it was the problem of transport, rather than inclination, that was holding back the rate of emigration from the northern countries before the 1860s. Temporary emigration did become established in Britain by the 1880s at the latest, and it was becoming important in Scandinavia at the same time (Erickson, 1980, *325–6*; Norman and Rundblom, 1988, *107*; Tederbrand, 1976, *209–10*). We must therefore be careful not to overestimate the differences between northern Europe in the middle of the nineteenth century and southern and eastern Europe some forty years later. There may have been a drop in temporary emigration because there was less opportunity to return, not because there was no reason for it.

We might expect that emigration from Ireland, where the people remained both rural and poor, would have had a large temporary component. Yet over the whole period the Irish were less likely to return than any other emigrants except the Jews. Irish emigration was also different in another respect. It included almost equal numbers of males and females. One reason for this pattern was the timing of Irish emigration. In the years when very large numbers of Irish were leaving – the 1840s and 1850s – the emigrants went by sailing ship. When emigrants went by steamship in the later nineteenth century, there were fewer Irish left to travel on them. But even in the later nineteenth century, there were few temporaries among Irish emigrants. There was also a high proportion of single women. There were probably two main reasons. First, prospects for women were poor in Ireland since there was little industry and after the Famine only a limited number of the rural population married. This meant that many women had no option but to work on a farm – often that of a relative. The second reason was that Irish women, being largely literate and also English-speaking, were at an advantage in the United States in both the labour and marriage markets. A puzzle remains, however. Poor prospects were not unique to Ireland. One suggestion why there was so little temporary emigration from Ireland is that the Irish were 'voluntary exiles' who would not return because of reasons connected with the Famine and the Anglo-Irish connection. For example, it is likely that the Famine, by making potato cultivation undesirable, permanently altered the output of Irish agriculture and reduced the demand for labour (Jackson, 1988, *1007*; Miller, 1985, *556*; Solar, 1989, *128*).

The changes in the character of emigration towards the end of the nineteenth century were of great political importance in the United States. In the years before the First World War two-thirds of American immigrants were coming from southern and eastern Europe. The 'new' immigrants, as they were called, were compared to the 'old' to the disadvantage of the former. The most important vehicle for this view was the Dillingham Commission which was active from 1907 to 1910 (Jones, 1960, *177–83*; Taylor, 1971, *239–50*). The argument against the 'new' immigrants rested on two assumptions. In the first place, the 'new' immigrants were undesirable because they included a high proportion of young single adults and because they had a high rate of return. There are many questions of fact and interpretation here which will be discussed below.

The second assumption was that the new immigrants had not made a rational decision to go to the United States, but had been induced to do so by the activities of shipping companies or had been recruited by labour contractors. The issue turns on what was meant by 'induced' or 'recruited'. We know very little about the activities of shipping companies and shipping agents. But the papers of a Swedish company (Larssons) that have survived show that their marketing was not aggressive. The literature that Larssons sent out was not persuasive. It was largely confined to the conditions that the emigrant might expect on the journey, and the

United States was hardly mentioned. Studies of Italian emigration have come to similar conclusions (Brattne, 1976, *276, 285-9*; Curti and Burr, 1950, *211*). The fact that there were large regional disparities in emigration rates also argues that the ability of outside agencies to induce emigration was limited. For example, it would have been possible for shipping companies to sell tickets anywhere in Italy, yet some very poor regions had low emigration. This suggests that the agents were following, not leading, the market for emigrants.

It is also thought that the direct recruitment of labour in Europe by American companies was largely ineffective. Charlotte Erickson showed that the practice of importing workers on contract into the United States had stopped even before 1885 when it became illegal (Erickson, 1957, *88-105*). The reason was that recruiting contract labour was usually more trouble than it was worth, not least because it was easy for immigrants to break the contracts if they thought that they were being exploited. To some extent, American immigrants were protected by the sheer size of the American labour market and its competitiveness. This was not necessarily true in other countries.

Most emigrants did not have to depend on intermediaries like shipping agents or labour contractors because they had the assurance of personal contacts. Emigration agents, of whatever kind, provided an additional and useful source of information, but it was not usually the critical source. We can be fairly sure that few people emigrated against their better judgment.

7

Assisted emigration

Emigration was actively promoted by governments, railways and land companies. But only a minority of the emigrants were affected, the great majority paying their own fare. If emigrants were 'assisted', they were more likely to be helped by friends and relatives than by outside agencies. A reasonable guess is that about a quarter of the emigrants were helped by friends or relatives and only some 10 per cent were officially assisted.

Emigrants had frequently been discouraged by European governments in the early nineteenth century. Policy was guided by mercantilist principles, which held that labour was a national resource and that the national 'wealth' would fall if labour was lost. Even the British banned the emigration of skilled artisans at one time. Prohibitions on emigration were not easy to enforce, however. After some years governments began to see that emigration would be a way of relieving poverty and removing undesirables. They began to promote emigration schemes. By mid century, however, the desire to emigrate in most western European countries was strong and the schemes were abandoned as unnecessary. Government policy then shifted towards protecting the emigrants from exploitation by shipping companies and emigration agents (Norman and Rundblom, 1988, 42–4). British government schemes continued, nevertheless, because they had the additional aim of populating the colonies. Emigrants were to be induced to go to the Empire rather than elsewhere. Between 1846 and 1869, 339,000 emigrants from Britain and Ireland were aided by government schemes, but this was only 7 per cent of all emigrants at that time (Glass and Taylor, 1976, 59–98).

The abandonment of European emigration schemes meant that

the initiative passed to government or quasi-government agencies in countries that were competing for immigrants. Many of the programmes were aimed at agricultural colonisation. Two well-known examples are the attempt by railroad companies to settle Swedish emigrants in northern Minnesota in the 1860s and 1870s and the Canadian government scheme between 1896 and 1914 which led to the settlement of Manitoba, partly by 200,000 Ukrainians (Ljundmark, 1971, *263–66*; Marr and Patterson, 1980, *349–55*). If a settlement scheme reduced the total cost of emigration for individuals, we would expect that the rate of emigration would increase. But a more important effect was probably to divert the emigrants from one destination to another, for example from Iowa to Minnesota. We must also remember that the Minnesota scheme was successful partly because Swedish immigrants were already living in Minnesota. Canadian agents failed to induce Swedes to settle in Canada where there was no existing Swedish settlement. The Canadian government also found it very difficult to recruit agricultural labourers in Britain in the 1860s and 1870s (Horn, 1972, *97*).

Governments in remote countries had little choice but to subsidise the cost of the passage if they wanted to attract immigrations. The aim in Australia and New Zealand, for example, was to divert British and Irish emigrants from the United States and Canada (Pope, 1985, *48–51*). About 45 per cent of all Australian immigrants before the Second World War were assisted in some way, in addition to the 146,000 convicts who came between 1788 and 1850 (Jackson, 1988, *26*). Assisted passages to Australia tended to be offered only in periods of full employment. It was found that subsidising immigrants was politically impossible in periods of depression as, for example, in the years after 1893. Fluctuations in the subsidy led to wide variations in the rate of immigration into Australia which showed how important assisted passages were and how remote Australia was from the mainstream of emigration.

Another well known example of assisted emigration is the São Paulo scheme. In the late nineteenth and early twentieth centuries, the government of São Paulo recruited workers under contract to work in the coffee plantations; 806,000 were assisted, or a half of all immigration into São Paulo province. The scheme was expensive for the provincial government and the cost was not borne by the main beneficiaries – the landowners – because they paid little taxation (Gould, 1980b, *279–80*). Two-thirds of the immigrants were Italians. Conditions on the coffee plantations were so bad that in 1907 the Italian government, by the Pirinetti decrees, banned the activities of recruiting agencies. Emigration to Brazil fell immediately, and returns to Italy increased. Consequently, the Brazilian agents began to recruit in Japan (Foerster, 1919, *91*; Gould, 1980b, *274*). This episode should enable us to test whether assistance increased the rate of emigration or whether it merely altered the destination of people who had already decided to leave. Unfortunately for our test the Brazilian coffee boom broke at the same time as the Italian government introduced the Pirinetti decrees. As in the Australian case, the degree to which the emigrants were 'induced' to go to Brazil or were 'diverted' there remains elusive.

8
Emigration and urban growth

One of the most important controversies in the history of European emigration is the relationship between emigration and urban growth. The growth of urban areas created economic opportunities in Europe and, potentially, an alternative destination for rural emigrants. Their main choice then became a move to a city in an overseas country or to one in their own country. Some writers have argued that the growth of European cities determined the emigration rate. If the pressures to emigrate occurred in the rural areas some of the pressure could be absorbed by a rural-urban move within the country. If urban growth was insufficient to absorb the migrants the remainder emigrated (Thomas, 1954, *124–8*; Jones, 1960, *45–6, 60–2*). For example, high emigration rates from Italy and Ireland have been linked to their relatively small urban populations.

The German case is very interesting. There was a marked decline in emigration from Germany after the 1880s which has been linked with rapid urbanisation and, in particular, with the industrialisation of the Ruhrgebiet and Saxony. After the 1880s, emigration from western Germany virtually ceased and most migrants from east of the Oder moved internally (2,200,000 net of returns, 1871–1910 compared with 1,000,000 emigrants). By 1900, Germany had become a country of net immigration. There were 1,000,000 foreign workers in 1914 (Bade, 1985, *124–5*; 1987, *141*; Walker, 1964, *189–91*).

The opposite occurred in Britain. Emigration increased as the country became more urban and industrialised. It is possible that the contrast between the German and British experience is related to the growth of GNP. The German economy was growing faster than the British in the late nineteenth century. Hence jobs in the urban areas in Germany were created at a faster rate. But a study of English and Welsh migration (1861–1900) does not support this explanation. The study found that the urban areas in England and Wales did exert a powerful attraction on the rural population, but their effect on the rate of emigration was limited. This may have been a consequence of chains that pulled people in the direction of emigration (i.e. the labour market was segmented). Alternatively, emigration may have been more attractive than internal migration even when we discount for the additional cost and risk (Baines, 1986, *213–49*). Another possibility is the Germans could have maximised their income by emigration but *chose* not to do so. Studies of Swedish emigration have also failed to find any systematic relation between internal migration and emigration (Ostergren, 1986, *132*).

The view that urban growth was the main determinant of the rate of emigration is an important component of the idea of an 'Atlantic economy'. This idea derives from the identification of 'long swings' of 18–20 years duration in growth rates, capital movements, migration and other variables in several countries (Easterlin, 1968, *342*). Brinley Thomas identified alternating 18–20 year cycles in the growth of the urban areas in some European countries and in the main destination countries: the United States, Canada and Australia. In one phase of the cycle, e.g. in the 1870s, the urban areas in Europe grew relatively faster than did urban centres overseas. The demand for labour was increasing faster in Europe. Hence rural-urban migration in Europe was relatively high, and emigration was relatively low. In the subsequent phase, e.g. in the 1870s, the urban areas in the destination countries grew relatively faster than did towns in Europe. Thus there was a fall in rural-urban migration in Europe and a rise in emigration. The link was provided by swings in the direction of investment. In the first phase, relatively more was invested in housing and social overhead capital in the European cities. In the second phase, relatively more was invested overseas, thus creating jobs which in the previous decade had been created in Europe. There has been some disagreement about the dynamic mechanism in the swings. For example, the direction of capital movements could be exogenous, or the prime mover could be exogenous movements in the rate of population growth, although the latter seems unlikely (Thomas, 1954, *92*, *124–5*, *175*; 1972, *45–54*).

The view that the migration pattern of European and overseas countries was determined by cycles of investment in the urban areas depends on an assumption that the majority of the European emigrants came from the rural areas. Rural-urban migration and emigration would then have been substitutes. Recent research is beginning to modify this view. By the end of the nineteenth century the average emigration rates from the urban areas in Norway, Finland, Denmark and Britain were *higher* than from the rural areas. Emigration rates from some German, and probably from some Italian cities, were also high relative to those from the rural areas (Baines, 1986, *143–7*; Hvidt, 1975, *41*, *52*; Kero, 1974, *54*; Semmingsen, 1972, *53*).

These data must be interpreted with caution. Most of the evidence, for example that taken from the Danish emigration contracts, is based on returns of the emigrants' 'place of last residence'. It is possible that the urban emigrants had been born in a rural area, moved to an urban area and subsequently emigrated. This proposition is difficult to test because data sets showing the place of birth as well as the place of last residence are rare. But there is enough direct and indirect evidence, particularly in Scandinavia, to show the existence of 'stage-emigration' as the phenomenon is called. For example, less than half of the emigrants from Bergen in 1875–94 had been born there and only 25 per cent of those from Stockholm (1880–93) (Nilsson, 1973, *365*; Semmingsen, 1960, *154*).

Scandinavian historians have developed the idea of the 'urban influence field'. Some of the rural areas near the larger cities had relatively low emigration rates. Migrants from these rural areas initially went to the large cities. Some subsequently emigrated. Urban influence fields have been identified for Bergen, Oslo, Stockholm, Göteborg, Malmö, Norrköping, Helsinki, Tampere, Turku, Copenhagen and St Petersburg. On the other hand, the smaller and more remote towns did not have urban influence fields and their emigrants tended to emigrate directly overseas (Norman and Rundblom, 1988, *81*; Hvidt, 1975, *58*; Rondhal, 1972, *269*; Rundblom and Norman, 1976, *134–6*; Kero, 1974, *54*).

The idea of stage emigration brings us back to the question of the migration decision. Was it taken in a rural or in an urban environment? The answer is important because it relates to the problem of the 'centre' and the 'periphery'. How realistic is it to think of emigrants as people who thought that they were outside the mainstream of economic development? Did they feel, for example, that their occupations were threatened by technological change? Of course, we can never know what was in their minds. Nor can we know where the emigrants were living when they made the decision to leave. If the urban-rural stage emigrants had already decided to leave the country before they moved to an urban area they were, in effect, rural emigrants. The length of time that urban emigrants had been living in the urban area should be used as a proxy, however. If they had lived in the city for only a few months we can assume that their decision to leave had already been made before they moved to the city. They may have stayed in the city only to earn the passage money. A study of emigration from Stockholm in the years 1880–93, which were years of high emigration, does not support this view, however. Three-quarters of the emigrants from Stockholm had not been born there. But nearly half had lived in Stockholm for more than five years and 40 per cent of the stage emigrants had come from another town. Hence, in this case we can assume that the decision to emigrate from Stockholm must have been affected by urban influences and the city was unlikely to have been a reservoir for essentially rural migrants (Nilsson, 1973, *310*). A study of a small industrial town in northern Sweden for a longer period came to similar conclusions (Tederbrand, 1972, *308*). Unfortunately, these studies depend on tracing individuals from one period to another and suitable data are scarce. We know very little about this issue, particularly for countries other than Sweden. A further complication is that between 1881 and 1911 the majority of Swedish emigrants, and stage emigrants, were women. This is unlikely to be true of other countries (Norman and Rundblom, 1988, *79*). It would be fair to say that the so-called 'through traffic issue' had not been resolved.

The English migration study, which we have discussed, was also able to estimate the number of emigrants from the cities who had been born in the rural areas. In the period 1861–1900, no more than 40 per cent of the rural emigrants could have been stage emigrants. This is on a generous assumption that people who had gone to the city were twice as likely to emigrate as those who had not. The main finding of the study was that *all* English emigration was dominated by the cities. About half of the English and Welsh emigrants in this period had been born in cities and large towns. Hence, if we include some of the stage emigrants, the majority of the emigration decisions must have been made in an urban environment (Baines, 1986, *260–5*). About 22 per cent of all emigrants came from London in this period, of whom at least three-quarters had been born in that city. Three-quarters of Stockholm's emigrants in the 1880s had not been born there. English emigration, in particular its urban character, was obviously very different from that of other European countries – or at least from those that we know about.

We should be careful, however. The definition of stage emigration that most historians use is a very narrow one. Their argument is that people who moved from a rural to an urban environment were more likely to emigrate than those who had not, either because they had already decided to go, or because they were converted to emigration while they lived in the city. It is possible, however, that all internal migrants, not just those who went to the cities, were more likely to emigrate. Alternatively, some internal moves may have affected the decision to emigrate, but not others. Would we expect the experience of harvest migration for example, to have had as great an effect as a move to the capital city (Rundblom and Norman, 1976, *163*)? Finally, at what point was a decision to emigrate most likely to be made? For obvious reasons, these hypotheses are virtually impossible to test.

9

The economic effects of immigration

The estimation of the effect of immigration on the growth of an economy is not easy. Put in the simplest possible terms, the effect depends on the relative abundance of other factors of production (capital and resources), and whether the economy is open or closed – i.e. whether the economy has a high level of exports and imports. If there were no countervailing factors, immigration would increase the income of the actual immigrants but would be expected to lower average incomes in those areas of the economy that immigrants were entering. Hence average incomes in the economy would fall, or would not rise as fast as they would have done if there had been no immigration (Greenwood and McDowell, 1986, *1745–50*; Spengler, 1958, *37–44*). This is the most commonly used argument in favour of restricting immigration, particularly if the immigrants were likely to come from a country with a lower standard of living. The American quota system which was introduced in the 1920s and the 'White Australia Policy' which was the dominant principle of Australian legislation until the 1960s were, in part, reactions of this fear.

The balance of evidence suggests that immigration did not reduce the rate of growth of income in the regions of recent settlement in the nineteenth century and possibly as late as the First World War. There were a number of reasons for this. Periods of immigration were usually associated with an increase in the demand for exports which meant that output could expand rapidly. Most important, there were increasing returns to scale in many areas. Output per head, and output per unit of capital, could rise, largely because resources were abundant and labour scarce. Hence when immigrants entered an industry, production costs tended to fall, as happened when Polish immigrants entered the Pittsburg steel mills in the early twentieth century. Of course, many immigrants entered unproductive and low-paid jobs where there were few economies of scale, as was the case with many services in the urban areas. But these were the sort of jobs that had to be done by someone. Immigration allowed other workers to be upwardly displaced from these jobs into sectors that did have increasing returns.

The ability of the destination countries to absorb immigrants without average incomes falling also depended on their ability to increase investment. Investment ratios tended to be high in these countries in any case because, among other things, there was a need for social overhead capital, such as an extensive railway system. But the high level of investment needed to absorb the immigrants was not a problem. Periods of high immigration corresponded to periods when capital imports from Europe were also high. This was true of Argentina and Australia in the 1880s and Canada in the 1900–14 period. In the 1880s for example, Argentina and Australia were importing 45 per cent of their net capital investment.

The British capital market specialised in lending to the regions of recent settlement. Hence the rate of immigration into these countries depended partly on Europe's ability to absorb their imports and partly on Britain's ability to lend overseas. In turn, this depended on the rate of growth of income in Europe and the willingness of the European governments to allow a high level of imports. The latter varied. In Britain the economy was completely open to imports between 1860 and 1914. The high propensity to import in Britain in this period was a critical factor in the growth of the export economies and in their ability to maintain a high level of income despite a high level of immigration. Even the United States remained a net capital importer until the early twentieth century, although by that time growth was not dependent on foreign investment, or on overseas trade (Foreman-Peck, 1983, *102–6, 127–33, 155–6* Kenwood and Lougheed, 1983, *103–15, 143–6*).

Immigration is likely to have had different effects on unskilled and skilled workers and on profits. Again the calculation is complex. The effect depends on the degree of occupational segregation. For example, if large numbers of unskilled immigrants were entering at the bottom of the labour market, where economies of scale were low, and there was little upward mobility, the incomes of the other unskilled workers would fall. Costs would be reduced in that sector of the economy and profits would be increased. The skilled workers would also be better off because the costs of many of the products that they purchased would fall. This is probably what happened in the early twentieth century in the United States. In other words, the labour market was segmented and, as a result, the gap between the standard of living of the unskilled workers and the rest of the population was widened (Spengler, 1958, *35–6*; Williams, 1976, *319–20*). It is also likely that the unskilled labour market was segmented because the native workers were able to enforce discrimination against immigrants (McGouldrick and Tannen, 1977, *724, 741–3*).

We know that by the later nineteenth century the majority of immigrants were entering urban occupations. Yet, with the exception of the United States, the economies of the destination countries were still overwhelmingly dependent on agriculture in 1900. Even the USA still had 37 per cent of its population in agriculture at that time. What was the relation between agricultural expansion and urban growth? In the United States, for example, it used to be said that the possibility of setting up western farms provided a 'safety valve' which maintained relatively high incomes for the urban/industrial workers. This view has had to be modified. The cost of setting up a farm in the west after the Civil War has been estimated at $1000 plus the cost of the land. This amount was beyond the means of most of the urban population, native or immigrant. But there was an important relation between the rate of westward expansion and immigration. After all, they were two components of the same phenomenon, the growth of the American economy. The question can be posed differently. If the option of moving to a western farm had not been available, what would have happened to the sons and daughters of the American farmers? Presumably more of them would have migrated towards the cities, which is what happened in Europe. The rate of growth of urban income would have fallen or the rate of immigration would have fallen. In other words, we know that employers in the American cities could rely on yet more immigrants if they needed more labour. They had no reason to look elsewhere unless the supply of immigrant labour was interrupted or there was a large increase in demand. This occurred in the First World War. Northern employers were forced to look elsewhere for labour, which had the effect of starting links – i.e. 'chains' – that allowed far more blacks to leave the South and was the beginning of extensive black migration to the northern cities (Thomas, 1972, *141–7*).

There is a second issue, however. The immigrants may have been of different 'quality' from the native population. It is frequently said, for example, that immigrants were more enterprising than the people who remained in Europe. The argument is based on the view that emigration was a process which selected the more enterprising and also on the success of many immigrants in their adopted countries. We have already discussed the view that the emigrants were deviant – which is not proven. Nor does the degree of success in another country tell us very much about the individual qualities of immigrants. 'Enterprise' can only be measured *ex post* not *ex ante*. Success was related to what it was possible to achieve. It does not tell us how other people – those who remained in Europe – would have fared in a new environment had they been the ones to go.

Skilled immigrants were also part of the transfer of European technology to overseas countries in the nineteenth century. There are many examples, including the pottery industry (Staffordshire to Paterson, New Jersey), wine (south Germany to South Australia), and textiles (Lancashire to New England). Skilled immigrants were important in technical transfer because, through most of the nineteenth century, the introduction of machinery needed individual attention. In the nineteenth century skilled immigrants, particularly British, were to be found in ironworks, mines and textiles in many parts of the world. Often this was because the decline of an industry in Europe had coincided with its rapid growth somewhere else. An example is provided by the decline of Cornish hard rock mining and the not unconnected rise of mining in Mexico, Michigan and Australia (Rowe, 1953, *326, 378*).

There are some important *caveats*, however. In the first place, European technology often required a great deal of adaptation. Wages were usually higher in the overseas countries and resources more abundant. A rational entrepreneur would be more likely to

introduce technology that saved labour than his European counter-
part (Jeremy, 1981, *148–9, 256*).

Immigration also had the effect of changing the age structure of
the labour force. Since there were always more young adults
among the immigrants, the labour force of the destination countries increased at a faster rate than the population as a whole. For
example, in Australia in 1861, the workforce was 51 per cent of the
population, whereas in Britain it was only 45 per cent. Hence if the
productivity of the Australians and the British had been identical,
Australian output per head of population would have been 3 per
cent higher (Jackson, 1988, *62*). It has been calculated that
between the 1880s and the First World War, a third of the growth
in the United States' labour force was because of immigration
(Williamson, 1974, *331*). Put another way, immigrants were not
undifferentiated units of labour. Even if they had no explicit skills,
the adult immigrants entered at the peak of their earning power.
They were a free gift of capital carrying with them the costs of their
upbringing. Hence the economy could achieve a higher rate of
capital investment. One estimate is that the United States gained a
minimum of five years' investment from immigration. Immigration
allowed the United States to achieve the capital stock of say, 1912,
in 1907 or earlier (Neal and Uselding, 1972, *84–8*). This calculation is fraught with problems. For example, the result assumes that
there was no trade-off between fertility and immigration. In other
words, it assumes that if there had been no immigration the native
population would have remained the same. This is discussed
below.

The relationship between immigration and changes in the
economy of the receiving countries could work both ways. Consider the effects of the southern and eastern European labour
market. We know that the wages of unskilled workers fell relative
to those of skilled workers in the early twentieth century. One
effect was that it became more profitable for American businessmen to invest in technology that could be used by unskilled
workers. The changes in the Ford automobile factories at the time
are a good example (Bodnar, 1985, *98*). Unskilled immigration
also affected the influence of the skilled workers. This was not
necessarily to their disadvantage. New technology often only
displaced the skilled workers upwards, into jobs that were not open

to unskilled immigrants. We can say that the heavy immigration of unskilled workers into the American urban areas in the late nineteenth and early twentieth centuries was both a cause and a consequence of changes in the American economy. The immigrants made it easier for technical change to occur and because technical changes did occur it became easier for immigrants to force their way into the bottom of the industrial labour market. In other words, it became easier to emigrate to the United States.

The effect of immigration on the growth of trade unions and other working-class institutions is difficult to assess. A general argument would run as follows. The entry of large numbers of unskilled workers would make it more difficult for others to form trade unions. On the other hand, a tight-knit immigrant group would have an advantage. The experience of the American cigar workers is probably typical, at least as far as the United States is concerned. Cigar manufacture was initially a skilled occupation undertaken in different cities by Belgian, German and British immigrants. It was well organised by American standards. In the early twentieth century, technical change made it possible to replace the skilled workers with unskilled, mainly female, immigrants and the solidarity of the skilled immigrant workers collapsed (Bodnar, 1985, *93*). On the other hand, in a country like Australia the history of trade unions was quite different. The solidarity of the Australian workers was not threatened by immigration as it was in the United States. Natives and immigrants were members of the same tight-knit immigrant group.

It may not have mattered to the economy whether immigrants to a particular receiving country came from one European country rather than another. But from a political point of view, it was very important. For example, it could be shown that the white dominions of the British Empire were of no economic advantage to Britain, in the sense that the British economy would have gained the same economic benefits from these countries if they had been foreign countries, rather as Britain benefited from the development of Argentina. Moreover, if the Empire had not existed Britain would have incurred fewer defence and other costs (Davies and Hutterbach, 1987, *303–6, 315–16*). But we do know that the Empire countries were only too willing to give military support to

Britain in 1914. From a political viewpoint, it did matter that the white dominions had been settled by British immigrants and not by immigrants from another European country. The same point could be made about the relation between Britain and the United States. However, the Anglo-American relationship was beginning to weaken in the late nineteenth century, as the later immigrants to the USA tended to dilute the British orientation.

It is easy to calculate the relative contribution of immigration and natural increase to the population growth of the destination countries. Immigration was not the most important component of population growth, even when the descendants of the immigrants are included. This calculation is rather arbitrary, however. The majority of the population of the destination countries, including all of the white population, was ultimately descended from immigrants. In the long run, virtually all population growth was the product of immigration. For the sake of argument, we can define the white population in 1840 as 'native'. We can also assume that there was no difference between native and immigrant fertility and mortality. These heroic assumptions allow us to calculate that only about 59 per cent of United States population growth would have occurred by 1940 had there been no immigration. The population of the United States would have been 85 million in 1940 instead of 132 million. The population of Canada would have been 9 million, of Argentina 8 million, and of Australia, which had little immigration before 1840, only 1 million. In 1940 the population of these countries was about 11, 15, and 7 million respectively. The population of the European countries would have been correspondingly greater. Consider an example of great historical importance. On these assumptions, the United States would probably have been the richest economy in the world in 1914 even if there had been no immigration after 1840. (We would have to make various assumptions about the causes of growth.) But it would probably have had a smaller population than Germany (Spengler, 1958, 26–7).

The contribution of immigration to population growth may seem surprisingly low. This is because of return migration which we know was high. In the case of Canada, it also reflects emigration to the USA. Return migration not only reduced the number of permanent immigrants but also of their descendants. There is another possibility, however. Immigration may have reduced fertility and mortality, particularly the latter. In the short turn, immigration increased the number of births because the immigrants were disproportionately young. But immigration could have reduced native fertility in the long run. The effect of immigration on final population size would then be muted. If births fell *pari passu* with immigration, then immigration would have had zero effect on the ultimate population size. This argument was common currency in the United States in the late nineteenth century. It was said that immigration was increasing competition in the labour market, reducing the prospects for native Americans. Therefore native Americans were having fewer children. This view was associated with the Superintendent of the Census, F. A. Walker, who wrote a famous paper in 1896. It had important political implications, not least because an increasing proportion of the immigrants were coming from southern and eastern Europe while the natives were usually of northern European extraction. As always, counterfactuals are difficult to evaluate. What we do know, however, is that native fertility in the United States had been in decline for most of the nineteenth century, long before the arrival of the 'new' immigrants. We also know that native fertility continued to fall even after immigration was curtailed in the 1920s (Shergold, 1974, *171*).

10
The family and assimilation

Recent years have seen a great increase in interest in the experience of the immigrants after they had arrived. Studies have refined our understanding of concepts such as 'ethnic ghetto' and 'assimilation' and have corrected some serious misconceptions about the immigrant experience in several countries. Many of the misconceptions related to the role of the family.

Historians of American migration frequently used to assume that the immigrants came from a Europe that was not only uniformly poor but had 'traditional' institutions that inhibited economic and social change. It followed that a move to the United States would be virtually the only way that a poor European could improve his or her economic condition. Because Europe was characterised as 'traditional', emigration was thought to have entailed a move away from the influence of the family. This was partly because immigration was seen as a component of the development of American capitalism which, in turn, was associated with the growth of individual as opposed to collective behaviour. Put another way, emigration was seen as a way in which enterprising individuals could escape the confines of the family or the village community. The immigrant family was 'uprooted' by the work patterns of capitalist America (Handlin, 1951).

The immigrant community in the new country was seen as a stepping stone from a 'traditional past' to a 'capitalist future' (Bodnar, 1985, *142*). Most emigrants who entered the cities – who were the majority by the later nineteenth century – came into an ethnic neighbourhood where many of the old beliefs and customs of Europe survived. But it was said that as they moved up the social and economic scale they tended to abandon most of their background and to 'assimilate' with the dominant culture. This view implied that successful immigrants or their descendants would leave the ghetto.

How far do these stereotypes fit the experience of the immigrants? In the first place, Europe was not unchanging in the nineteenth century. On the contrary, it was often *because* changes were taking place that emigration occurred. The notion that European immigrants to the United States were meeting capitalism for the first time is clearly wrong. They would not have been able to reach the United States without using capitalist institutions. Nor is it likely that the majority of emigrants had rejected the influence of their families. We have seen that a great deal of European emigration took place *because of* family connections and finance. Nor were emigrants an undifferentiated mass. Their composition reflected many of the social and economic divisions of Europe which were carried with them to the United States and other countries.

Perhaps the most interesting finding of the recent research about immigrant communities in the United States is that the family usually remained a central component of day-to-day life. There seems to have been relatively little tension between the 'traditional' demands of the family and the demands of modern capitalism. On the contrary, immigrants seemed to have used family connections to obtain employment in preference to the institutions of the new country, such as trade unions, political parties or social clubs (Bodnar, 1985, *71–83*; Briggs, 1978, *68*; Bukowczyk, 1987, *61–70*; Vecoli, 1986, *268, 292*; Yans-McLaughlin, 1977, *260–5*).

The idea that upward mobility was associated with a rejection of traditional values has also been seriously questioned. In the first place, it has been shown that immigrants did not improve their occupational status nearly as fast as had been commonly supposed. The great majority of second generation immigrants in the American cities that have been studied, for example the Boston Irish and the New York Italians, had similar occupations to those of their immigrant parents (Kessner, 1977, *114*; Thernstrom, 1973, *100, 115–19*). Many immigrants were able to become successful entrepreneurs, of course, but in a surprising number of cases they had been proprietors or businessmen before they left Europe. Hence, one of the reasons why entrepreneurs were commoner among some ethnic groups than among others was that some ethnic groups (i.e. the Jews) had a high proportion of small proprietors in Europe and some (i.e. the Italians) did not (Bodnar, 1985, *171*; Kessner, 1977, *80–2*). We should also remember that the success of most immigrant businessmen depended on their ability to serve the immigrant community. They frequently had no choice but to serve immigrants since they were often excluded from the established business community. In other words, most of the successful immigrants owed their success to immigrant traditions and institutions rather than to their ability to break with those traditions and assimilate to a new culture (Barton, 1975, *112*; Bodnar, 1985, *71– 83*). More recent events also give us a clue about the extent of 'assimilation'. If the immigrants had been 'assimilated' in the United States, why was there such a growth in ethnic consciousness in the 1970s?

The creation of a successful immigrant community may have depended on the cultural, social and economic traditions which the immigrants brought with them from Europe. It could also depend on the economic and social environment in the new country. Italian immigration provides a useful example. In 1914, about one-third of the 1,000,000 Italians living in Argentina were to be found in Buenos Aires and about 25 per cent of the 1,500,000 living in the United States were to be found in New York. The Italians in New York were not as successful as their compatriots in Buenos Aires. Nor did the former seem to be improving their position in the early twentieth century. The comparison is interesting because at least half of the Italians in Buenos Aires came from the richer north of Italy. The great majority of the Italians in New York came from the poorer and less literate south. The question is, did the southern Italians fare relatively badly in New York because they were southerners or because they went to New York? And if so, why did they not go to Buenos Aires? The most important difference, however, may have been that in Argentina the Italians were the dominant immigrant group (20 per cent of the population) and in some respects were more successful than the native Argentines. Italian emigration to Argentina was also of longer standing. In New York the Italians were only one of many groups and also one of the most recent arrivals. They had little choice but to enter low-paid jobs in services (Baily, 1983, *298–305*).

Our ideas about the ghetto have also had to be modified. Zunz and others have criticised the idea of a monolithic ghetto, replacing it with the concept of 'ethnic dominance'. Zunz accepted that the majority of the population of the 'little Italys' or 'Polish Hills' of the American cities were of Italian or Polish extraction. But the ghettos also included large numbers of immigrants from other countries and with different traditions. The ghettos were not the streets of Italian or Polish villages transported to Chicago or Pittsburg (Zunz, 1982, 59–87). There were also important regional differences among the immigrant groups, particularly the Italians. Although 75 per cent of the Italians in Chicago in 1900 were southerners, for example, there were representatives of nearly all Italian regions in the city (Vecoli, 1986, 268). Nor, in many American cities, did the majority of the immigrant groups live in one or two well-defined areas. This was not because there was a high degree of upward mobility, but because there was a high degree of residential mobility. Thernstrom used the term 'flowing proletariat' to describe this phenomenon (Bodnar, 1985, 175; Cinel, 1982, 106; Kessner, 1977, 143; Thernstrom, 1964, 96).

The relation between the immigrant rural communities in the United States and their European counterparts also seems to have been complex. They were not usually copies of European agricultural communities. Research on agricultural immigrants from both Sweden and Norway has suggested that the communities tended to remain 'traditional' in family relations and religious practices but divergent in economic matters. Also religion seems to have been a more important cultural characteristic of Scandinavian immigrants than their national origin. This may have been because the Swedish and Norwegian agricultural communities were set up relatively early. One of the reasons for emigration was the conservative desire to avoid social changes in Scandinavia that were thought undesirable (Gjerde, 1985, 139–41, 169–201; Norman and Rundblom, 1988, 272–3).

The experience of the majority of British immigrants was somewhat different. They had little need to 'assimilate' in the English-speaking countries although they were not above using immigrant networks (McCleary, 1984). There were no British ghettos in the United States, where the British were so widely distributed as to be 'invisible immigrants' – to use the title of a well-known book

(Erickson, 1972). In Australia, over 90 per cent of the population were of British or Irish origin from the middle of the nineteenth century until very recently (Jackson, 1988, 5, *38–40*). Social differences were less marked in Australia than in Britain but they still reflected social differences in the 'mother country'.

In conclusion, it is useful to think about 'assimilation' from the viewpoint of the individual. Sometimes immigrants relied on the new institutions of the destination countries. But family links and immigrant institutions remained powerful, and it was often more efficient for an immigrant to use them. It depended simply on which path he or she thought would be the most effective at the time. To an individual there was little conflict between 'traditional' and 'new' ways.

11
The end of mass emigration

Emigration in 1914 was at record levels but for obvious reasons there was little further emigration during the First World War. It picked up after the war, but never returned to its pre-war level in any country. This was most apparent in eastern Europe. Between 1925 and 1939, there were only 1,100,000 emigrants from the eastern European countries, very few of whom went overseas. This compared with 5 million emigrants to the United States alone between 1900 and 1925 (Zubrzyski, 1958, *227*). The fall in the rate of emigration had important effects in eastern Europe. Most of these countries remained predominantly agricultural in the 1920s but still had a high rate of population growth. Emigration had been an important safety valve.

There were several reasons why emigration rates fell. In the first place, the First World War had changed the international economy. For example, overseas investment in the regions of recent settlement was reduced together with their access to the European market (Foreman-Peck, 1983, *191–4, 198–205*). The most immediate change was the introduction of restrictions on both emigration and immigration which was connected with a rise of economic and political nationalism, the force of which had been increased by the First World War. The first sign of the new politics was the enforced redistribution of population following the Versailles settlement, including the relocation of 1 million Germans.

The introduction of immigration quotas by the United States in 1924 and 1927 was critical. The purpose of quotas was to reduce the total number of immigrants and to change their ethnic composition (Jones, 1960, *275–7*). The size of the annual quota depended on the stock of people of those 'national' (i.e. ethnic) origins in the

United States before the First World War. The effect, which was intended, was drastically to reduce immigration from southern and eastern Europe while leaving the door open for immigrants from northern Europe. The implication was that the immigrants from northern and western Europe had been of greater advantage to the host country than those from southern and eastern Europe, which, as we have seen, is debatable. Under the 1924 quota, only 160,000 immigrants from outside the Americas were allowed to enter the United States, of which 40 per cent were to be from the UK and a third from Germany. Quotas were further reduced in 1927 to 150,000, of which 55 per cent were to be from the UK and 15 per cent from Germany.

It was still possible for eastern European immigrants to enter other parts of Europe, Canada and Latin America, although there were some restrictions. But the capacity of these countries to absorb immigrants was less than that of the United States. Italian emigration was also curtailed except to France, which had become the main immigration country in Europe. Before the war, Germany had been the main European destination but the Weimar Republic imposed restrictions (Bade, 1987, *80, 141–2*). France accepted immigrants because she had an ageing population and had also lost a large proportion of her young adult population in the war. There was also a certain aversion to industrial employment among the native population (Green, 1985, *152–5*). 650,000 Italians, 450,000 Portuguese and similar numbers from eastern Europe entered France in the interwar period (net of returns) (Tederbrand, 1985, *358*).

Emigration was further reduced by the rise of totalitarianism in Europe. The Soviet and Hungarian governments were the first to curtail emigration, followed by Italy and Germany. Italy actually encouraged emigration until 1927 and then discouraged it. The further fall in emigration in the 1930s was not only a consequence of the further growth of restriction, however. In the early 1930s, there was a drastic fall in income in all the receiving countries. Emigration would have fallen even if there had been no restriction.

In the British Empire, as it was still called, there was an increase in politically motivated emigration schemes in the 1920s. Such schemes were necessary, as a 1922 Australian government statement put it, 'to keep Australia 98 per cent British' (Pope, 1981,

36). Under the Empire Settlement Act (1922) Britain agreed to pay up to half of the cost of assisted passages to Australia, New Zealand and Canada. The aim was *settlement* and precedence was given to families. Some orphans were also sent out, often in not too pleasant circumstances (Parr, 1980, *11, 40*). It was expected that the bulk of the immigrants to the white dominions would be absorbed into agriculture. This turned out to be a serious error. The world was already in excess supply of most agricultural products in the 1920s, and the 1930s were worse. Schemes like Empire Settlement could not be insulated from the effects of the depression on the domestic economies. In the economic depression the openings for new arrivals dried up and the dominion governments faced political pressures to curtail immigration. It is not surprising that many of the British emigrants of the 1920s returned.

Conclusion

Emigration was a very widespread phenomenon in the nineteenth and early twentieth centuries which makes it very difficult to explain. Several universal explanations have been offered, including the development of the international economy and the desire of individuals to improve their economic and social conditions. These explanations are true but trivial. They could apply to almost everything that was happening in the period.

The big problem is to explain the *incidence* of emigration – assuming that we are able to measure it. We may be able to explain to our own satisfaction the reasons for the emigration of one group. But what if an apparently similar group did not leave? The more we know about other regions, not to say other countries, the more partial our explanations become. But the comparative method, although difficult, is the one that yields the insights. In other words, it is *because* it is difficult to make generalisations about emigration history that it is an interesting and important subject.

We still have a lot to learn, including more about the basic quantities. For example, what was the relationship between internal migration and emigration? We also need more micro-studies – detailed analyses of the experiences of limited numbers of people. The traditional methods of the historian can tell us more about motivation, especially if they are fortified by some use of theory. But questions about motivation are notoriously difficult to answer. Historians and social scientists should not delude themselves about the many grey areas in the history of European emigration. If they do not know the answer, they should say so.

Select bibliography

K. J. Bade (1985) 'German emigration to the United States and continental immigration to Germany in the late nineteenth and early twentieth centuries' (in Hoerder).

K. J. Bade (ed.) (1987) *Population, Labour and Migration in Nineteenth and Twentieth Century Germany* (Berg, Leamington Spa). An important collection. Summarises, in English, important recent research by German scholars.

K. J. Bade, (1987) 'German emigration, continental immigration: the German experience past and present' (in Bade).

S. L. Baily (1983) 'The adjustment of Italian immigrants in Buenos Aires and New York, 1870–1914', *American Historical Review*, 88, 2. Argues convincingly why Italian immigrants to Buenos Aires were relatively more successful than those who went to New York.

D. E. Baines (1986) *Migration in a Mature Economy. Emigration and Internal Migration in England and Wales, 1861–1900* (Cambridge University Press). Detailed quantitative analysis of the origins of England and Welsh emigrants. Shows, contrary to much previous writing, that emigration was predominantly urban and that stage emigration was comparatively rare.

J. J. Barton (1975) *Peasants and Strangers. Italians, Rumanians and Slovaks in an American City, 1890–1950* (Harvard University Press, Cambridge, Mass.).

C. Bobinska and A. Pilch (eds) (1976) *Employment Seeking Migrations of the Poles World Wide. XIXth and XXth Centuries* (Polonia Educational Research Centre). Considers Polish emigration, both overseas and within Europe, from an ethnically Polish perspective. 'Poland' was not a nation state between 1815 and 1919.

J. Bodnar (1985) *The Transplanted. A History of Immigrants in Urban America* (Indiana University Press). Very fine summary of the last 20 years' research on the immigrant experience in the USA. This research has corrected many misconceptions about 'assimilation' and 'modernisation' and re-emphasised the role of the family and immigrant institutions. (See Barton, 1975; Briggs, 1978; Bukowczyk, 1987; Cinel, 1982; Kessner, 1977; Thernstrom, 1973; Yans-McLaughlin, 1977; Zunz, 1982).

B. Brattne (1976) *Broderne Larsson. En Studie i Svensk Emigrant Agent Verksamet inder 1880 Talet.* (The Larsson brothers. A study of the activity of Swedish emigrant agencies during the 1880s) (Almqvist and Wiksell, Uppsala). (English summary.) One of the very few studies of the activities of emigration agents. Shows that, in the main, the Larssons did not persuade people to emigrate; 100,000 people had corresponded with them and not emigrated.

C. B. Brettell (1986) *Men who Migrate, Women who Wait. Population and History in a Portuguese Parish* (Princeton University Press). Study of society in northern Portuguese villages which depended on the income of temporary emigrants to Brazil.

J. Briggs (1978) *An American Passage. Immigrants to Three American Cities, 1890–1930* (Yale University Press, New Haven). Questions cultural explanations of immigrant behaviour in the USA. For example, the poor education of Italians was not because they did not value education but because they found it difficult to obtain.

J. J. Bukowczyk (1987) *And My Children Did Not Know Me. A History of the Polish-Americans* (Indiana University Press).

S. Carlsson (1976) 'Chronology and composition of Swedish emigration to North America' (in Rundblom and Norman).

J. Chmelar (1973) 'The Austrian emigration, 1900–14', *Perspectives in American History*, 7.

D. Cinel (1982) *From Italy to San Francisco. The Immigrant Experience* (Stanford University Press). Includes useful discussion of conditions in Italy. Argues, following Coletti's famous book of 1912, that access to land was a critical factor in emigration.

I. Cismic (1986) 'Emigration from Yugoslavia prior to World War II' (in Glazier and De Rosa).

R. L. Cohn (1984) 'Mortality on immigrant voyages to New York, 1836–53', *Journal of Economic History*, 54.

B. Collins (1982) 'Irish emigration to Dundee and Paisley during the first half of the nineteenth century', in Goldstrom, J. M. and Clarkson, L. A. (eds), *Irish Population, Economy and Society. Essays in Honour of the late K. H. Connell* (Oxford University Press).

M. Curti and K. Burr (1950) 'The immigrant and the American image in Europe, 1860–1914', *Mississippi Valley Historical Review*, 37. Classic article about information. Overestimates the direct effect of agents and recruiters on the decision to emigrate.

L. Davies and R. A. Hutterbach (1987) *Mammon and the Pursuit of Empire*

(Cambridge University Press). Heroic effort to estimate the costs and benefits of Empire to Britain, with implications for emigration.

L. Di Comite (1986) 'Aspects of Italian emigration, 1881–1915' (in Glazier and De Rosa).

R. A. Easterlin (1968) *Population, Labour Force and Long Swings in Economic Growth: the American Experience* (NBER, Columbia University Press). Standard treatment of the causes and consequences of fluctuations in fertility, investment and international migration.

D. Eltis (1983) 'Free and coerced trans-Atlantic migration. Some comparisons', *American Historical Review*, 88.

C. Erickson (1957) *American Industry and the European Immigrant* (Harvard University Press, Cambridge, Mass.). Shows that the practice of importing immigrants under contract to American companies had become unimportant long before it became illegal in 1885.

C. Erickson (1972) *Invisible Immigrants. The Adaptation of English and Scottish Immigrants in Nineteenth Century America* (Weidenfeld & Nicholson, London). Uses letters to build up a picture of English immigrants in the United States – a group that was so dispersed as to be 'invisible'.

C. Erickson (1972) 'Who were the English and Scottish emigrants in the 1880s?' In Glass, D. V. and Revelle, R. (eds), *Population and Social Change* (Arnold, London). A very influential article. In this and subsequent papers, Professor Erickson pioneered the use of the ships' lists to analyse the characteristics of British emigrants in much greater detail than hitherto.

C. Erickson (ed.) (1976) *Emigration from Europe, 1815–1914. Select Documents* (Adam and Charles Black, London).

C. Erickson (1980) 'The English' in Thernstrom, S. (ed.), *The Harvard Encyclopedia of American Ethnic Groups* (Harvard University Press, Cambridge, Mass.).

C. Erickson (1986) 'The use of passenger lists for the study of British and Irish emigration' (in Glazier and De Rosa).

C. Erickson (1989, 1990) 'Emigration to the USA from the British Isles Part I: Emigration from the British Isles. Part II: Who were the English emigrants?' *Population Studies*, 43 and 44.

I. Ferenczi and W. Willcox (eds) (1929–31) *International Migrations* (NBER, New York). Two volumes. Remains the most important collection of raw data. Their view – common in the 1930s – that European emigrants had been 'pushed' has been completely discredited.

D. Fitzpatrick (1984) *Irish Emigration* (Economic and Social History Society of Ireland, Dublin). A very short introduction.

R. F. Foerster (1919) *The Italian Emigration of our Times* (Harvard

University Press, Cambridge, Mass.). Classic description of Italian emigration, stressing the high rate of return.

J. Foreman-Peck (1983) *A History of the World Economy. International Economic Relations since 1850* (Harvester, Brighton).

J. M. Gandar (1979) 'New Zealand net migration in the latter part of the nineteenth century', *Australian Economic History Review*, 19. The timing of New Zealand immigration was unusual. In some periods, for example, the country had net emigration.

J. Gjerde (1985) *From Peasants to Farmers. The Migration from Balestrand, Norway to the Upper Mid-West* (Cambridge University Press). One of several recent books which use a range of evidence to draw out in great detail the relationship between immigrant communities in the United States and the corresponding European communities. They show that the former were not mere copies of the latter.

D. V. Glass and P. A. M. Taylor (eds) (1976) *Population and Emigration in Nineteenth-Century Britain* (Irish University Press, Dublin). Government documents mainly concerning the first half of the century when the government was more involved.

I. A. Glazier and L. De Rosa (eds) (1986) *Migration Across Time and Distance. Population Mobility in Historical Context* (Holmes & Meier, New York). Very useful collection of conference papers, emphasising the reasons for leaving Europe.

J. D. Gould (1979) 'European inter-continental emigration, 1815–1914: patterns and causes', *Journal of European Economic History*, 8. This and the two following references are a very important series of articles. Discussion of regions, 'chains', 'diffusion' and other important questions. Particularly good on Italian emigration.

J. D. Gould (1980a) 'European inter-continental emigrations, 1815–1914. The road home: return migration from the USA', *Journal of European Economic History*, 9.

J. D. Gould (1980b) 'European inter-continental emigration. The role of "diffusion" and "feedback"', *Journal of European Economic History*, 9.

N. L. Green (1985) 'Filling the void. Immigration to France before the First World War' (in Hoerder). France was a country of net immigration in this period.

M. J. Greenwood and J. M. McDowell (1986) 'The factor market consequences of US immigration', *Journal of Economic Literature*, XXIV. The best recent summary of the economic effects of immigration. Technically difficult.

O. Handlin (1951) *The Uprooted* (Harvard University Press, Cambridge, Mass.). Famous study which argued that immigrants had to make a complete break from their European background in order to succeed in the United States. Now discredited.

M. L. Hansen (1940) *The Atlantic Migration, 1607–1860* (Harvard University Press, Cambridge, Mass.). One of the first studies to try to see emigration from the viewpoint of the individual emigrant.

J. R. Harris and M. P. Todaro (1970) 'Migration, unemployment and development: a two sector analysis', *American Economic Review*, 60. Theoretical analysis of a dual labour market, including search costs.

J. Higham (1955) *Strangers in the Land. Patterns of American Nativism, 1860–1925* (Rutgers University Press). A classic study. The recent second edition is virtually unaltered.

D. Hoerder (ed.) (1985) *Labour Migrations in the Atlantic Economies. The European and North American Working Class during the Period of Industrialisation* (Greenwood Press, Westport, Conn.). Contains several convenient summaries of earlier work, some not previously available in English.

P. Horn (1972) 'Agricultural trade unionism and emigration, 1872–1881', *Historical Journal*, 15.

K. Hvidt (1975) *Flight to America. The Social Background of 300,000 Danish Emigrants* (Academic Press, New York). Detailed examination of *all* Danish emigrants in the period. Based on the discovery of a unique data set in the Royal Library of which the author was Librarian.

F. E. Hyde (1975) *Cunard and the North Atlantic, 1840–1973. A History of Shipping and Financial Management* (Macmillan, London). One-third of all European emigrants to the United States passed through the port of Liverpool, 1860–1900. Cunard was the most important carrier.

R. V. Jackson (1988) *The Population History of Australia* (Penguin Books, Ringwood, Vic.).

D. J. Jeremy (1981) *Transatlantic Industrial Revolution. The Diffusion of Textile Technologies between Britain and America, 1790–1830s* (Blackwell, Oxford). Questions the importance of technical transfer by immigrants. Technical transfer did need the skills of British immigrants but the American technology was not dependent on British technology.

M. A. Jones (1960) *American Immigration* (Chicago University Press). Still useful account of immigration from an American viewpoint. Includes a good survey of nativism and the Dillingham Commission.

M. A. Jones (1973) 'The background to emigration from Great Britain in the nineteenth century', *Perspectives in American History*, 7.

W. D. Kamphoefner (1986) 'At the crossroads of economic development. Background factors affecting emigration from nineteenth century Germany' (in Glazier and De Rosa).

W. D. Kamphoefner (1987) *Transplanted Westphalians. Chain Migration from Germany to a Rural Mid-Western Community* (Princeton University Press).

R. E. Kennedy (1974) *Ireland: Fertility, Emigration and Marriage since the Famine* (University of California Press, Los Angeles).

A. G. Kenwood and A. L. Lougheed (1983) *The Growth of the International Economy, 1820–1980* (Allen & Unwin, Sydney).

R. Kero (1974) *Migration from Finland to North America in the Years between the United States Civil War and the First World War* (Yliopisto Turun, Turku). Very full analysis of Finnish emigration including comparison with other Scandinavian countries.

T. Kessner (1977) *The Golden Door: Italian and Jewish Mobility in New York City, 1880–1915* (Oxford University Press). Very influential book about relative social mobility.

W. Kollman and P. Marshalk (1973) 'German emigration to the USA', *Perspectives in American History*, 7.

J. Kosa (1957) 'A century of Hungarian emigration, 1850–1950', *American Slavic and East European Review*, 16.

J. Knodel (1974) *The Decline of Fertility in Germany, 1871–1939* (Princeton University Press). Considers the relationship between emigration and fertility change.

F. Krajlic (1985) 'Round trip Croatia, 1900–14' (in Hoerder).

S. Kuznets (1975) 'Immigration of Russian Jews into the United States. Background and structure', *Perspectives in American History*, 9. Argues that despite persecution, Jewish emigrants to the United States were selected in favour of those occupations that were most likely to prosper.

M. Livi-Bacci (1961) *L'immigrazione e l'assimilazione degli Italiana negli Stati Uniti secundo la statistiche demografische Americana* (Guiffre, Milan).

L. Ljungmark (1971) *For Sale Minnesota. Organised Promotion of Scandinavian Immigration, 1866–73* (Scandinavian University Books). Shows that the success of the scheme depended on the prior settlement of Swedish immigrants.

L. Ljungmark (1979) *Swedish Exodus* (Swedish Pioneer Historical Society, University of Southern Illinois Press).

B. L. Lowell (1987) *Scandinavian Exodus. Demographic and Social Development of Nineteenth Century Rural communities* (Westview Press, Boulder, Colo.).

W. L. Marr and D. G. Patterson (1980) *Canada, an Economic History* (Gage).

J. S. Macdonald (1963) 'Agricultural organisation, migration and labour militancy in rural Italy, 1902–13', *Economic History Review*, 16. A much quoted article, which raises the question that emigration and radical politics were substitutes, depending on whether land could be obtained by purchase.

G. F. Macleary (1984) 'Networks among British immigrants and accommodation to Canadian society, 1900–14', *Histoire Sociale/Social History*, 18. Very little has been written about how British immigrants made their way in their new country.

P. F. McGouldrick and M. B. Tannen (1977) 'Did American manufacturers discriminate against immigrants before 1914?' *Journal of Economic History*, 38.

K. A. Miller (1985) *Emigrants and Exiles. Ireland and the Exodus to North America* (Oxford University Press). Asks why so few Irish emigrants returned. Suggests that it was the trauma of the Famine. Or it may have been because the real Ireland was not the 'Emerald Isle' that the 'exiles' had constructed for themselves.

B. R. Mitchell (1980) *European Historical Statistics, 1750–1975* (Macmillan, London).

B. R. Mitchell (1983) *International Historical Statistics. The Americas and Australasia* (Macmillan, London).

T. Moe (1970) *Demographic Developments and Economic Growth in Norway, 1740–1940. An Econometric Study* (Arno Press, New York). Probably the best of the 'determinants of migration' models.

J. Mokyr (1983) *Why Ireland Starved. A Quantitative and Analytical History of the Irish Economy, 1800–1850* (Allen & Unwin, London). Pioneering attempt to place the Famine in the context of the Irish economy. Full of insight but some serious analytical flaws.

E. Morawska (1985) *For Bread with Butter. The Life Worlds of East Central Europeans in Johnstown, Pennsylvania, 1890–1940* (Cambridge University Press, New York). Good discussion of the eastern European background, especially the reasons for the high rate of migration within Europe.

L. Neal (1976) 'Cross-spectral analysis of long swings in Atlantic migration', in P. Uselding (ed.), *Research in Economic History*, Vol. 1 (Greenwich, Conn.). Includes one of the best appraisals of the 'determination of migration' models which were very popular in the 1970s. Technically very difficult.

L. Neal and P. Uselding (1972) 'Immigration, a neglected source of American economic growth, 1790–1912', *Oxford Economic Papers*, 24. Quantifies the additional cost to the American economy if the growth in the labour force through immigration had come through native births.

F. Nilsson (1973) *Emigrationen från Stockholm till Nordamerika, 1880–93* (Studia Historica Upsaliensis). English summary. A careful analysis of, among other things, the 'through traffic issue'. Were the emigrants who went from Stockholm rural emigrants or did they decide to emigrate when they were living in a city?

H. Norman (1976) 'Causes of emigration. An attempt at a multivariate analysis' (in Rundblom & Norman).

H. Norman and H. Rundblom (1985) 'Migration patterns in the Nordic countries' (in Hoerder).

H. Norman and H. Rundblom (1988) *Transatlantic Connections. Nordic Migration to the New World after 1800* (Norwegian Universities Press, Oslo).

B. Oden (1972) 'Scandinavian emigration prior to 1914, *Scandinavian Economic History Review*, 20. Includes a discussion about the effect of changes in passage costs on the rate of emigration.

C. Ó Gráda (1989) *The Great Irish Famine* (Macmillan, London). Very good summary but says surprisingly little about emigration.

R. C. Ostergren (1986) 'Swedish migration to North America in Transatlantic perspective' (in Glazier and De Rosa).

R. C. Ostergren (1987) *A Community Transplanted; the Trans-Atlantic Experience of a Swedish Immigrant Settlement in the Upper Mid-West, 1835–1913* (University of Wisconsin Press). Suggests that the 'transplanted community' may have adapted to the institutions of the new country in economic matters but maintained traditional ties in family and church matters.

M. Palairet (1979) 'The "New" immigration and the newest; Slavic migration from the Balkans to America and industrial Europe since the late nineteenth century', in T. C. Smout (ed.), *The Search for Wealth and Stability. Essays in Economic and Social History Presented to M. W. Flinn* (Macmillan, London).

J. Parr (1980) *Labouring Children. British Immigrant Apprentices to Canada, 1869–1924* (Croom Helm, London).

M. J. Piore (1979) *Birds of Passage. Migrant Labour and Industrial Societies* (Cambridge University Press).

D. Pope (1981) 'The contours of Australian immigration, 1901–30', *Australian Economic History Review*, 21. Recalculates Australian immigration statistics. Shows that there was net emigration in the 1890s.

D. Pope (1985) 'Some factors inhibiting Australian immigrants in the 1920s', *Australian Economic History Review*, 24.

C. W. Price (1963) *Southern Europeans in Australia* (Oxford University Press, Melbourne). Pioneering study of chain migration. Most examples post-Second World War.

J. Puskas (1986) 'Hungarian migration patterns, 1880–1930; from macro-analysis to microanalysis (in Glazier and De Rosa).

B. Rondhal (1972) *Emigration Folke Emflyttning och Sasongarbete i att Saguvarks-distrikt i Sodra Haslinghand, 1865–1910* (Almqvist &

Wiksell, Stockholm). English summary. An excellent example of a detailed local study which shows the complexity of the migration decision. The study by Tederbrand is equally good.

P. Roudie (1985) 'Long distance emigration from the port of Bordeaux', *Journal of Historical Geography*, 11. Interesting example of an emigration port which did not see many French emigrants.

J. Rowe (1953) *Cornwall in the Age of the Industrial Revolution* (Liverpool University Press).

H. Rundblom and H. Norman (eds) (1976) *From Sweden to America. A History of the Migration* (University of Minnesota Press, Minneapolis and Acta Universitatis Upsaliensis). The key publication of the (quantitative) Uppsala Project. Includes the famous maps showing emigration rates from Scandinavian countries by county.

T. Saloutos (1956) *They Remembered America. The Story of the Repatriated Greek-Americans* (University of California Press, Berkeley).

A. Schrier (1959) *Ireland and the American Emigration, 1850–1900* (University of Minnesota Press, Minneapolis).

I. Semmingsen (1960) 'Norwegian emigration in the nineteenth century', *Scandinavian Economic History Review*, 7. These papers summarise Professor Semmingsen's pioneering work on the detailed causes of Norwegian emigration.

I. Semmingsen (1972) 'Emigration from Scandinavia', *Scandinavian Economic History Review*, 20.

I. Semmingsen (1978) *Norway to America. A History of the Migration* (University of Minnesota Press, Minneapolis).

A. Sen (1981) *Poverty and Famine. An Essay in Entitlements and Deprivation* (Oxford University Press).

P. Shergold (1974) 'The Walker thesis revisited. Immigration and white American fertility, 1800–60', *Australian Economic History Review*, 14. Investigates the view – current in the United States in the late nineteenth century – that immigration reduced the birth rate and hence merely replaced natives by aliens.

P. M. Solar (1989) 'The Great Irish Famine was no ordinary subsistence crisis', in Crawford, E. M. (ed.), *Famine, the Irish Experience, 900–1900* (John Donald, Edinburgh).

J. J. Spengler (1958) 'Effects produced in receiving countries by pre-1939 immigration', in Thomas b. (ed.), *The Economics of International Migration* (IEA, Macmillan, London).

R. P. Swierenga (1986) 'Dutch international migration and occupational change' (in Glazier and De Rosa).

R. P. Swierenga and H. S. Stout (1976) 'Social and economic patterns of migration from the Netherlands in the nineteenth century', in Uselding, P. (ed.), *Research in Economic History*, Vol. 1 (Greenwich, Conn.).

P. A. M. Taylor (1965) *Expectations Westward. The Mormons and the Emigration of the British Converts in the Nineteenth Century* (Oliver & Boyd, Edinburgh).

P. A. M. Taylor (1971) *The Distant Magnet. European Emigration to the USA* (Eyre & Spottiswoode, London). Particularly good on improvements in transport. Also contains an excellent collection of contemporary photographs by Lewis Hine.

L.-G. Tederbrand (1976) 'Remigration to Sweden' (in Rundblom and Norman).

L.-G. Tederbrand (1972) *Vasternoeland och Nordamerika, 1875–1913* (Studia Historica Upsaliensa, 42; Almqvist & Wiksell, Uppsala). English summary.

L. G. Tederbrand (1985) 'Re-migrants from America to Sweden' (in Hoerder).

S. Thernstrom (1964) *Poverty and Progress in a Nineteenth Century City* (Harvard University Press, Cambridge, Mass.). Very influential book concerning the social mobility of immigrants and native-born over more than one generation.

S. Thernstrom (1973) *The Other Bostonians: Poverty and Progress in the American Metropolis, 1880–1970* (Harvard University Press, Cambridge, Mass.).

F. Thistlethwaite (1960) 'Migration from Europe overseas in the nineteenth and twentieth centuries', *XIe Congrès International des Sciences Historiques, V; Histoire Contemporaine* (Almqvist & Wicksell, Stockholm). A paper that attempted to re-direct research towards the European background of the emigrants. Very influential in Scandinavia.

B. Thomas (1954) *Migration and Economic Growth. A Study of Great Britain and the Atlantic Economy* (NIESR, Cambridge University Press). Draws out a sophisticated relationship between population growth, domestic and overseas investment and internal and overseas migration. Some modification of the thesis has been necessary but it is still very influential.

B. Thomas (1972) *Migration and Urban Development. A Reappraisal of British and American Long Cycles* (Methuen, London).

W. I. Thomas and F. Znaniecki (eds) (1918) *The Polish Peasant in Europe and America* (Knopf, New York; abridged edition, University of Illinois Press, Urbana, 1984).

R. J. Vecoli (1986) 'The formation of Chicago's "Little Italies" (in Glazier and De Rosa).

K. Virtanen (1979) *Settlement and Return. Finnish Emigrants in the International Overseas Migration Movement* (Studia Historia, 10, Helsinki).

K. Virtanen (1985) 'Finnish migrants (1860–1930) in the overseas migration movement' (in Hoerder).

M. Walker (1964) *Germany and the Emigration, 1816–85* (Harvard University Press, Cambridge, Mass.). Still very useful. Includes discussion of German religious groups.

J. C. Williamson (1974) 'Migration to the New World. Long term influences and impact', *Explorations in Economic History*, 2. Surveys quantitative literature concerning European emigration.

J. C. Williamson (1976) 'American prices and urban inequality since 1820', *Journal of Economic History*, 36.

V. Yans-McLaughlin (1977) *Family and Community. Italian Immigrants in Buffalo, 1880–1930* (Cornell University Press).

C. C. Zimmerman (1955) 'American roots in an Italian village', *Genus*, XI.

J. Zubrzycki (1953) 'Emigration from Poland in the nineteenth and twentieth centuries', *Population Studies*, 6.

J. Zubrzycki (1958) 'Migration and the economy of eastern Europe', in B. Thomas (ed.), *The Economics of International Migration* (Macmillan, London).

O. Zunz (1982) *The Changing Face of Inequality. Urbanization, Industrial Development and Immigration in Detroit, 1880–1920* (Chicago University Press).

Index

New Studies in Economic and Social History

Previously published as

Studies in Economic History

Titles in the series available from the Macmillan Press Limited

Economic History Society

The Economic History Society, which numbers around 3,000 members, publishes the *Economic History Review* four times a year (free to members) and holds an annual conference.

Enquiries about membership should be addressed to

The Assistant Secretary
Economic History Society
PO Box 70
Kingswood
Bristol
BS15 5TB

Full-time students may join at special rates.